P9-CQY-997

Premarital Counseling

Premarital Counseling

by

H. Norman Wright

MOODY PRESS
CHICAGO

© 1977, 1981 by
THE MOODY BIBLE INSTITUTE
OF CHICAGO
Revised Edition

Revised Edition, 1982

All rights reserved. No part of this book may be reproduced in any form without permission in writing from the publisher, except in the case of brief quotations embodied in critical articles or reviews.

The use of selected references from various versions of the Bible in this publication does not necessarily imply publisher endorsement of the versions in their entirety.

Library of Congress Cataloging in Publication Data

Wright, H. Norman.
Premarital counseling.

Bibliography: p. 83, 227-31
1. Marriage counseling—United States. I. Title.
HQ10.W73 1981   362.8'286   81-11214
ISBN: 0-8024-6812-8   AACR2

13 14 15 16 Printing/BB/Year 94 93 92 91 90

Printed in the United States of America

OVERTON MEMORIAL LIBRARY
HERITAGE CHRISTIAN UNIVERSITY
P.O. Box HCU
Florence, Alabama 35630

Contents

1

The Status of
Marriage Today

Literature is saturated with articles describing the plight of the American style of marriage and family. From *Ladies' Home Journal* to the *New Yorker*, *Christianity Today* to *Moody Monthly*, editors, educators, sociologists, anthropologists, politicians, and ministers are voicing their concern. If one is not convinced that difficulties exist, he has not been reading, has not been in touch with people, or is an idealist!

In 1972 the "Report on the American Family" by *Better Homes and Gardens* revealed that 71 percent of more than 340,000 participants believed that "American family life is in trouble."[1] Eighty-nine percent thought that most couples were not well prepared for marriage, and 85 percent thought that religion had lost its influence on family life today.

In a similar survey conducted in 1978 with 302,000 participants, 76 percent believed that American family life is in trouble and 72 percent felt that religion has lost its influence upon family life. Twenty-five hundred professional family educators and marriage counselors participated in the National Alliance for Family Life Research; a consensus of their opinion was: "There is a definite need for strengthening family life in this nation at the present time."[2] This same group was asked, "Do you feel that, overall, young people are receiving adequate preparation for marriage from their parents?" Ninety-three percent said no. If they are not receiving this preparation at home, then where are they being prepared?

Are people happy being married today? It is difficult to know, for various reports and specialists differ. Eighty percent of the participants in the *Better Homes and Gardens* study stated that most people they knew were happy in their marriages. A few years ago, *Life* magazine gave a similar statistic. Yet Dr. J. A. Fritz, in his book *The Essence of Marriage*, has suggested that marriages could be classified into four categories: happy, good, agreeable, and tolerable. He estimates that 5 percent would fall in the happy category, 10 percent in good, and the remaining 85 percent in the last two categories. Dr. James Peterson, professor of sociology at the University of Southern California, made a study of couples who had been married for twenty years or more. He discovered that of every one hundred such couples, only five could be classified as happy.

People today are concerned about marriage. Changes are taking place in family structure and in the permanency of marriage. In 1870 there were twenty-seven divorces for every 1,000 marriages in the United States.

In the May 15, 1978 issue of *Newsweek* magazine, the following information concerning marriage and divorce was given. The report, entitled "The Marriage Odds," indicated that 96 percent of all Americans will marry, and 38 percent of that group will divorce. Of those who divorce, 79 percent of them will remarry and 44 percent will divorce again.[3]

The attitude toward marriage today was revealed in the office of a marriage counselor when a young woman said, "When I got married I was looking for an ideal but I married an ordeal and now I want a new deal!" A recent cartoon in the *Los Angeles Times* pictured a pastor performing a wedding, and instead of the usual "till death do you part," he said, "till divorce do you part." This is not entirely unreal. Actual consideration has been given to this very question by Alvin Toffler in *Future Shock*. Toffler said, "As conventional marriage proves itself less and less capable of delivering on its promise of lifelong love, therefore, we can anticipate open public acceptance of temporary marriages."[4]

Margaret Mead suggested "an apprentice period for people

contemplating marriage, a five-year terminal point for all marriages with the option of either renewal or cancellation of the contract, and specially trained, government financed substitute parents for the children of dissolved marriages." Another suggestion is a "two level system with the first level of marriage limited to a five year period with no children allowed and then either cancellation of the contract or renewal to a permanent nondissolvable relationship and children allowed."[5]

Dr. Carl Rogers, in his book *Becoming Partners: Marriage and Its Alternatives*, said,

> To me it seems that we are living in an important and uncertain age, and the institution of marriage is most assuredly in an uncertain state. If 50-75 percent of Ford or General Motors cars completely fell apart within the early part of their lifetimes as automobiles, drastic steps would be taken. We have no such well organized way of dealing with our social institutions, so people are groping, more or less blindly, to find alternatives to marriage (which is certainly less than 50 percent successful). Living together without marriage, living in communes, extensive child-care centers, serial monogamy (with one divorce after another), the women's liberation movement to establish the woman as a person in her own right, new divorce laws which do away with the concept of guilt—these are all gropings toward some new form of man-woman relationship for the future. It would take a bolder man than I to predict what will emerge.[6]

The problem is not with the institution of marriage. The problem lies with the individuals within that structure and their attitudes toward it. Richard Lessor wrote, "In the twentieth century it is not a matter of marriage having been tried and found wanting. Marriage is deeply wanted but largely untried."[7] Today, in place of exerting consistent effort and determination to make one's marriage work, the solution is to "bail out." In certain counties of southern California, the ratio of marriages to divorces is now almost one to one.

Families are being disrupted not only by divorce.

> According to the Federal Bureau of Investigation statistics, police across the nation receive more calls for family conflicts than for murders, aggravated batteries and all other serious crimes. The

category of family conflicts includes not only quarrels between husband and wife but also between parent and child.[8]

It has been reported that over fifty percent of all homicides committed are violent physical attacks by one member of a family upon another member of the same family.[9]

Concern over this problem is not limited to families; law enforcement officials are also involved.

In general, police don't like dealing with family quarrels because they don't know what to expect and frequently the calls prove to be dangerous. FBI statistics show that 22 percent of all police fatalities occur while investigating domestic disturbances.[10]

These events and transitions are bound to have some effect upon people in our society. Nathan Ackerman, a leading family psychiatrist, expressed it this way:

At present, anxiety about marriage and family is almost universal. On every hand, one sees nervous concern over teenage marriage, infidelity, divorce, loosening sex standards, women's lib, momism, the decline of parental authority, the anarchy of youth, and so on. One senses deepening disillusion—even despair—surrounding the value of family life.[11]

Statements such as the following do nothing to relieve the high level of anxiety: "In this day of uprooted persons and a world threatened with revolution, the ancient value most endangered seems to be the family."[12] William Wolf, a psychoanalyst as quoted by Toffler, said, "The family is dead except for the first year or two of child rearing."[13]

The ultimate depth of pessimism is seen in the words of Nathan Ackerman concerning the family situation:

I am a psychiatrist who has devoted a lifetime to studying emotional problems of family living. I have pioneered in the field of family therapy. From where I sit, the picture of marriage and family in present-day society is a gloomy one. Family life seems to be cracking at the seams, and an effective mortar is nowhere available.[14]

There is, however, an effective mortar: the person of Jesus

Christ. The presence of Christ, the ministry of the Holy Spirit, and intense effort and work dedicated to the application of Scripture can bring stability, growth, and mutual satisfaction into a marital relationship.

Of all the changes occurring today, four are quite significant in relationship to the future of marriage.

The first change to consider is the movement toward the nuclear family as compared to the traditional extended family, or family of orientation. We have rejected the extended family of the past, the family from which one has come—one's own grandparents and parents. The closeness is no longer there except in rural areas. In America we emphasize separating ourselves from the parents. Little loyalty or obligation is felt toward them. There were many healthy aspects to the way families lived in close proximity to each other in the past. The arrangement gave a person or family someone to depend on. To be sure, the nuclear family unit has its strengths, but it has many problems as well.

A Canadian publication, *Hope for the Family*, said,

> Families have become small isolated, mobile, self-contained units. Very few societies today provide so little support for new parents as our society. As one author put it: "Young parents today are like the pioneers, alone in a wilderness, threatened by uncertainties, no rules but the ones they make themselves." Cut loose from relatives and traditions, families have become an easy target for the mass media.[15]

Professor Norman Ashcraft, anthropologist at Adelphi University, suggested:

> Psychiatrists call the "normal" family by a technical term, the "nuclear family," to refer to that supposedly tightly knit unit of father, mother and children. To the family repairmen, the harmonious nuclear family is the only way to live—especially in suburbia. It is right here that I take issue with these so called experts. For I believe that the suburban nuclear household, even in the best of circumstances, does not afford a healthy or happy life. It does not provide stable and emotionally satisfying relationships in the home, nor an environment that children want to live in. In fact, the more we have isolated this domestic unit behind the walls of the suburban home, the more we have alienated children from their parents—and husbands from their wives.[16]

Many believe that American family life is accurately portrayed by the nuclear family model of a father working, a mother at home, and children in school.

The changes in the structure of American family life can be seen in the US Bureau of Labor Statistics.

Life-style	Percent
Cohabitating couples and experimental families	4
Nuclear families with both parents working outside the home	16
Nuclear families with no wage earner	1
Nuclear families with one wage earner	13
Single parent families	16
Single, separated, divorced, widowed parents	21
Childless or post-child-rearing marriages	23
Extended families	6

The Bible states in Genesis 2:24: "For this cause a man shall leave his father and his mother, and shall cleave to his wife; and they shall become one flesh." Notice an emphasis on two verbs: leave and cleave. The word *leave* means to abandon, forsake, to sever one relationship before establishing another. Although the attachment to home and parents should be replaced by the attachment to one's mate, this does not mean disregarding or dishonoring one's parents but rather breaking the tie to one's parents and assuming responsibility for one's spouse.

The fifth commandment states, "Honour thy father and thy mother: that thy days may be long upon the land which the LORD thy God giveth thee" (Exod. 20:12). The same command is repeated in Ephesians 6:1-3. To honor is to "regard with high public esteem, to show the spirit of respect and consideration."[17] Honoring parents means to acknowledge them with respect as people to whom one is indebted more than he could ever repay.

Cutting off oneself from relatives, having no regard for the insight and opinions of parents or other family members, not showing concern for the physical well-being of older parents and grandparents—all contradict the teaching of the Word of God. Christians must evaluate what they are doing and why they are doing it in light of the Bible. In the area of relationships with relatives, it appears that families have moved away from biblical teaching. Young people would gain insight into and greater understanding of family relationships if they had a wider experience with other family members. All the experiences of growing up are going to affect one's future marriage.

A second change that developed in our society is that the choice of a mate is left entirely to the individuals involved. Years ago parents were directly involved. It is evident that people strive for independence today. However, we are not arguing the merits of the former system. There is something to be said for individual choice. But choices seem to be made on the romantic ideal of love based on feelings. As we shall see later, this is an unhealthy basis.

Dr. David Mace, a family life sociologist, has pointed out that marriage has changed from an institution to a companionship arrangement. It is also easier to get out of this arrangement than to get out of a book-of-the-month club. External pressure will not keep a couple together today. There must be internal cohesion. The question is, Is romantic love sufficient?

Love is necessary, but many people have an inadequate concept of what it is. Perhaps a typical definition can be expressed in this homespun statement: "Love is a feeling you feel when you feel that you're going to get a feeling that you never felt before!"

What about common interests, common background, vocational goals, spiritual similarities? What about liking the other person as a friend and enjoying his or her company? What about liking to work with the person over an extended period of time? Being a friend to one another fills many of the needs that people bring into marriage. There are many elements that should go into the selection of a mate, but too many people bypass them.

California has moved to counteract the problem of immature decisions to marry by requiring a court order for permission to marry when one or both persons are under the age of eighteen. Some countries also require premarital counseling for these couples. It would be good if in the future the requirement for premarital counseling would be advanced to all under twenty-one.

Have evangelical churches required and provided mandatory premarital counseling for any who seek marriage? In a 1972 survey of ninety-five churches, only twenty-five required counseling; fifty admitted to giving very limited counseling or none at all!

A third major change today is that marriage has moved from a relationship of partners with fixed roles to a relationship of partners with fluid roles. Husbands and wives fill many different and unique roles. Two of the most noted writers in the secular field, Wilbur Lederer and Donald Jackson, have stated that one of the elements most destructive to the marital relationship is the failure of spouses to identify, determine, and mutually assign areas of competence and responsibility—who is in charge of what. They feel it is important that the spouses deliberately and mutually develop rules to guide their behavior.[18]

Couples also have moved from a one-vote system to a two-vote system. Within this change it appears that married women have gained more power and assertiveness, and in many cases there is a crippling of male authority at home. Perhaps some women have taken over because of the abdication of men who have turned their energy toward their work. The responsibility for governing American households on a day-to-day basis has fallen largely upon the women.

Nowhere else in the world do women have more real decision-making power than their husbands than in the United States. They have economic power, religious power, and, because of the divorce laws, the power to easily dissolve the marriage.[19] Albert McClellan, in his book *New Times*, stated: "Family life has become mother-centered, with a sharing of responsibility by father and mother, and a decline in the role of the father as the family authority."[20] The parental role is a peripheral role for the American male.

This ambiguity of male authority is a result of the cult of independence, which eventually led to an attack upon the traditional authority of fathers and husbands. It is also partially due to the industrial life of our nation. Lawrence Fuchs states in *Family Matters* that the ambiguity of male authority is perhaps *the most striking and important characteristic of the American family system.* Our American culture places a high premium upon performance in work outside the home; this further undermines male dominance in the home. Some of those outside pressures to perform at work are so great (or the men claim the pressures are so great) that men welcome an escape from the responsibility of being the authority at home.[21] Leonard Benson, in his work

Fatherhood, goes so far as to say, "The American father is almost invisible, perhaps even at home."[22]

Striving for material success has been part of the reason for the absenteeism of father from the family. In some homes, the mother and children pressure father for more material goods. In others the father himself desires the comforts and gadgets that more money can bring (despite the time payments!).

Our culture has been described in the following manner:

> The success of the religion of consumption is self-evident. North Americans are consumption mad. Many people go around believing that without things they will simply disappear. North Americans are pleasure minded, self-indulgent, materialistic, and selfish.
>
> This vision has captured the hearts of many Christians, young and old. Many Christians try to live according to two visions—to enjoy the best of two worlds—to remain Christians while at the same time pledging to uphold the faith of consumption. Sooner or later, however, one vision, one spiritual force, will gain the upper hand, will become the directing, the determining force in our lives (Luke 12:29-31).[23]

Vance Packard, in the dedication of his book *The Waste Makers,* said: "To my mother and father, who have never confused the possession of goods with the good life."[24] Very few have this philosophy today. To many men, their job is their way of life and their self-image is deeply affected by their ability to provide for their family.

Nathan Ackerman vividly expressed this situation:

> The father strives mightily to show success as a man. He pursues what has been called "the suicidal cult of manliness." To prove his merit, it is not enough to be a man; he must be a superman. In his daily work, he serves some giant industrial organization, or he is a lone wolf in the jungle warfare of modern competitive enterprise. The more he succeeds, the more he dreads failure. He brings his work worries home. Depleted by his exertions, he has little emotional stamina left over to give freely of his love to wife and children.
>
> He wants to be buttressed for the war of tomorrow, but he finds his wife absorbed in her own busy life. He feels deserted and alone and angry that his wife gives him so little understanding. She

> reproaches him for not taking a more responsible role in the family. She demands more consideration for herself and the children. For the difficulties with the children she feels guilty. But she denies this guilt and projects it to father. Father takes it. He thinks it must really be his fault. Though confused and angry, he appeases mother because of his need for her. He tries to be useful to win her favor.[25]

This is true not just of those in secular work but also of those in Christian service. Many pastors are so involved in their work that their role in the family is nonexistent. There are many who boast that they have not had a day off in months and that they work seventy to ninety hours each week. That situation is nothing to boast about: it is sick!

A final change is in sexual morality. Much has been written on this subject; it is enough to say that the sexual behavior evident today, both in and out of marriage, threatens family stability, and is also a symptom of other problems.

A recent survey makes this point with graphic finality. The October 1975 issue of *Redbook* magazine presented the results of a survey concerning women's sexuality and sexual behavior. The report was based on surveys completed by 100,000 women. Results indicated that the likelihood that a young woman will have intercourse before marriage has been steadily increasing over the last ten years. For example, 69 percent of the women in this survey who were married prior to 1964 experienced premarital relations. Among those married after 1970, the number was 90 percent. The surveys also revealed that the strongly religious woman was more likely than other women to remain a virgin until marriage, but the influence of religion was less inhibiting than might be expected.[26] For those who have convictions and moral standards, prior sexual involvement can affect the marriage unless the total forgiveness of Jesus Christ is experienced.

In the midst of all these changes, the church can have an impact. Imagine what would happen if every couple who married in the next ten years experienced six to eight hours of premarital counseling in their local church and also spent thirty-five hours of outside preparation through books and tapes. This idea is the message of this book.

NOTES

1. "Report on the American Family." Published by *Better Homes and Gardens* (September 1972), pp. 7, 36, 137.
2. *National Alliance for Family Life Newsletter* (Spring 1973), p. 1.
3. *Newsweek*, 15 May 1978, p. 67.
4. Alvin Toffler, *Future Shock* (New York: Random House, 1970), p. 251.
5. From *Cherishable: Love and Marriage*, by David W. Augsburger. Copyright 1971 by Herald Press, Scottdale, Pa. Used by permission.
6. Carl Rogers, *Becoming Partners: Marriage and Its Alternatives* (New York: Delacorte, 1972), p. 11.
7. Richard Lessor, *Love & Marriage & Trading Stamps* (Niles, Ill.: Argus, 1971), p. 7. Reprinted with permission of Argus Communications.
8. Vida Deen, "Family Conflict Calls a Major Police Concern," *Santa Ana Register* (28 March 1973).
9. William Lederer in *Marriage: For and Against* (New York: Hart, 1972), p. 137.
10. Deen, "Family Conflict."
11. Nathan Ackerman in *Marriage: For and Against* (New York: Hart, 1972), p. 12.
12. Albert McClellan, *New Times* (Nashville: Broadman, 1969), p. 69.
13. William Wolf as quoted in *Future Shock* (New York: Random House, 1970), p. 238.
14. Ackerman, p. 12.
15. A. DeGraaff et al., *Hope for the Family* (Toronto: Wedge, 1971), p. 11.
16. Norman Ashcraft, "The Isolated, Fragile Modern Family," *Los Angeles Times* (21 May 1973).
17. William Hendricksen, "Ephesians," in *New Testament Commentary* (Grand Rapids: Baker, 1967), p. 259.
18. William Lederer and Donald Jackson, *The Mirages of Marriage* (New York: Norton, 1968), pp. 248-49.
19. Lawrence H. Fuchs, *Family Matters* (New York: Random House, 1972), pp. 27-28.
20. McClellan, p. 70.
21. Fuchs, p. 26.
22. Leonard Benson, *Fatherhood—A Sociological Perspective* (New York: Random House, 1968), p. 3.
23. DeGraaf, pp. 33-34.
24. Vance Packard, *The Waste Makers* (New York: McKay, 1974), Dedication.
25. Excerpted from pp. 110-15 from *The Psychodynamics of Family Life: Diagnosis and Treatment of Family Relationships*, by Nathan W. Ackerman, New York: Basic Books, 1958.
26. Robert and Amy Levin, "Sexual Pleasure: The Surprising Preferences of 100,000 Women," *Redbook* (October 1975), pp. 51-58.

2

Helping to Take the Risk out of Mate Selection

A young man came in one morning and said, "It's not worth it! I see so many of my friends' marriages breaking up, I'm never getting married. Marriage appears to be such a gamble—and it's the only game in town where both players can lose! There's too much risk involved in getting married! I don't want to end up a statistic." Perhaps he was running scared and being a bit overcautious. Yet his concern is echoed by many young people. In some cases this attitude lends itself to the move toward simply living together.

There is a risk involved in the marriage process, but the essential element is not so much finding the right person as it is becoming the right person. Both individuals can lose in the game of marriage, but it is just as possible for both to win!

Most couples are not fully aware of the complexity and dimensions of the marital relationship. Marriage means sharing in many areas of life such as:

- *Emotional*—a sharing of the emotional and fantasy levels of life.
- *Economic*—a sharing of the accumulation, use, and distribution of money.
- *Recreational*—a sharing of recreation and pleasure. Sharing involves not only recreation together but sharing your spouse for recreation with his or her own set of companions.

19

- *Social*—a sharing of social and interpersonal activities. Some enjoyed together and some enjoyed separately.
- *Geographical*—Saving space, time, and geographical proximity.
- *Sexual*—a unique sharing of the physical, sensual, and sexual aspects of two people.
- *Legal*—a couple's involvement in the civil and legal process of a society.
- *Religious*—Sharing beliefs, values, and traditions.

What is involved in the process of selecting a mate? What factors, conscious and unconscious (some have said that all couples in love are unconscious), move people toward one another? What does the evangelical church have to say to a young person about his choice of a life partner? Do we say that God has one person that He has selected to be your mate, or is there an unlimited stockpile that you could select from and still be within God's will? Often the church says only that a believer must marry a believer. That is scripturally true, but there are more factors involved in the selection of a mate than spiritual oneness.

REASONS FOR MARRIAGE

There are numerous reasons for marriage apart from being in love. *Pregnancy* is still a reason for marriage. In fact, about one-fourth of all marriages occur when the bride is pregnant. Probably many of these marriages would not have occurred had the woman not been pregnant. Research on these marriages shows a relationship between a premarital pregnancy and unhappiness in marriage.[1] In God's grace, these marriages do not have to end in a higher divorce rate or have a greater rate of unhappiness than others; the forgiveness of Jesus Christ can affect this situation as well as any other.

Rebound is a reason for marriage when a person attempts to find a marriage partner immediately after a relationship terminates. In a sense it is a frantic attempt to establish desirability in the eyes of the person who terminated the relationship. Marriage on the rebound is questionable because the marriage occurs in reference to the previous man or woman and not in reference to the new person.

Rebellion is a motivation for marriage and occurs in both

secular and Christian homes. This is a situation in which the parents say no and the young person says yes. This is a demonstration of one's control over one's own life, and possibly an attempt to demonstrate independence. Unfortunately, a person uses the marriage partner to get back at parents.

Escape from an unhappy home environment is another reason for marriage. Some of the reasons given are fighting, drinking, and molestation. This type of marriage is risky, as the knot-tying is often accomplished before genuine feelings of mutual trust, respect, and mature love have had any opportunity to develop.

Loneliness is a reason that stands by itself. Some cannot bear the thought of remaining alone for the rest of their days; they do not realize that a person can be married and still feel terribly lonely. Instantaneous intimacy does not occur at the altar, but must be developed over months and years of sharing and involvement. The flight from loneliness may place a strain upon the relationship. One person may be saying, "I'm so lonely. Be with me all the time and make me happy." The problems stemming from this attitude are apparent.

Physical appearance is a factor that probably influences everyone to some degree or another. Our society is highly influenced by the cult of youth and beauty. Often our standards for a partner's physical appearance are set not so much to satisfy our needs, but simply to gain the approval and admiration of others. Some build their self-concept upon their partner's physical attributes.

Social pressure may be direct or indirect and can come from many sources. Friends, parents, churches, schools convey the message, "It is normal to be married; to fit the norm you should get with it." On some college campuses a malady known as "senior panic" occurs. Engagement and marriage may be a means of gaining status; fears of being left behind are reinforced by others. In some churches when a young unmarried pastor arrives, matchmaking becomes the order of the day. Some churches will not hire a minister unless he is married; thus a young minister must either marry before he is ready to or desires to or spend months looking for a church.

Guilt and pity are still involved in some marriages. Marrying a person because one feels sorry for him or her because of physical defects, illness, or having a poor lot in life does not make a stable marital relationship.[2]

What about *romance?* Aren't love and romance a factor? Yes, but it is important to distinguish between genuine love and romantic love. Romantic love has been labeled cardiac-respiratory love. This is love with an emphasis upon excitement, thrills, and palpitations of the heart! Some people react as though there were a lack of oxygen in the area. Ecstasy, daydreaming, a deep physical yearning, and an apparent fever are all indications of this malady. Not only is this type of love blind, it is also destructive. Past or future is not taken into consideration in evaluating the potential of the relationship. Dr. James Peterson has aptly described the dangers of marriage for this reason:

> First, romance results in such distortions of personality that after marriage the two people can never fulfill the roles that they expect of each other. Second, romance so idealizes marriage and even sex that when the day-to-day experiences of marriage are encountered there must be disillusionment involved. Third, the romantic complex is so short-sighted that the premarital relationship is conducted almost entirely on the emotional level and consequently such problems as temperamental or value differences, religious or cultural differences, financial, occupational, or health problems are never considered. Fourth, romance develops such a false esctasy that there is implied in courtship a promise of a kind of happiness which could never be maintained during the realities of married life. Fifth, romance is such an escape from the negative aspects of personality to the extent that their repression obscures the real person. Later in marriage these negative factors to marital adjustment are bound to appear, and they do so in far greater detail and far more importantly simply because they were not evident earlier. Sixth, people engrossed in romance seem to be prohibited from wise planning for the basic needs of the future even to the point of failing to discuss the significant problems of early marriage.

It is difficult to know how pervasive the romantic fallacy really is. I suspect that it creates the greatest havoc with high school seniors or that half of the population who are married before they are twenty years old. Nevertheless, even in a college or young adult population one constantly finds as a final criterion for marriage the question of being in love. This is due to the distortion of the meaning of a true companionship in marriage by the press, by the magazines, and by cultural impact upon the last two or three generations. The result is that more serious and sober aspects of marital choice and marital expectations are not only neglected but sometimes ridiculed.[3]

MATE SELECTION

Ask college students the question, Why do most people get married? and one usually still receives the answer, because of romantic love, or people are destined to marry each other, or they just have this attraction for one another and marriage is the logical outcome. One fact that is often overlooked is that marriage partners need to fulfill certain qualifications to be suited to each other. In reality, however, more couples are thrown together by factors other than romance or the logic of intelligence!

There are many limits on mate selection. Physical location is the most significant limitation, a fact that seems highly unromantic.[4] The farther two people live apart, the more intervening opportunities there are to choose someone else. There is a limit to how much time and money a man will spend traveling to see a woman when there are other women closer by. Occasionally romantic love breaks all barriers, but those cases are the exception.

Research studies regarding marriage indicate that persons marry with greater than chance frequency within their own social class.[5] Any overall tendency for people to marry either "up" or "down" in social class is negligible.

When a person marries, does he choose a person just the opposite of himself? For years the statement "opposites attract" has been used to explain part of the attraction process. And yet the results of hundreds of studies of married couples indicate that, almost without exception, in physical, social, and psychological characteristics the mates were more alike than different. The exceptions, or those that appear to be exceptions, do not alter this overall tendency.

Within the framework of like marrying like, however, some characteristics appear to be quite opposite in each spouse. Since the fulfillment of needs is at the heart of much of mate selection, one will find that some needs in couples are complementary whereas some are contradictory.

It is in the area of complementary characteristics and needs that the concept "opposites attract" is seen to be somewhat accurate. The most important complementary needs involve dominance and submissiveness. If a person has a need to dominate he will tend to marry and be gratified by a person who needs to be submissive. If a man marries a woman who has the need to be dominant and he is submissive, there will be some conflict because the social expectations of our society call for the male to be dominant and the female to be submissive. In spite of social pressures, many couples choose to go against the expectation. If one has a need to nurture others, such as giving sympathy, love, protection, and indulgence, he would be happy with a partner who has the need to be nurtured. (Most people, fortunately, are capable of both, and that is healthier.) A person who needs to admire and praise others would enjoy being married to a person who needs to receive respect and admiration. If the needs of one spouse change years later, the relationship could be disrupted. Complementary needs help determine how two people treat each other.

It is important to keep in mind the distinction between complement and contradiction. Unfortunately, some couples label any difference between themselves as complementary. Complementary needs fit so well together that no compromise is required, whereas contradictory needs require a compromise on some middle ground, but not usually on a happy medium. For example, if one is extremely thrifty and the other is a big spender, the needs will clash head on. If one enjoys social contacts and the other is a recluse, conflict is almost inevitable.[6]

In our American culture people choose a partner whom they expect to be gratifying to them. It is interesting to note that both engaged and married couples see things in each other that cannot be found through testing. What an individual sees in another person is what pleases him. "What would ever attract him to that girl?" we ask, because we cannot see in her the things he sees. A couple's choice of each other is based upon a set of relationships pleasing to themselves, which they attribute to one another.

As people date and are attracted to one another, basic needs are met. Much of a couple's relationship is based upon the meeting of those needs. This means that there are literally thousands of people of the opposite sex who could fulfill those needs if the person has appropriate status qualities. Being held in esteem in someone else's eye confirms our worth in our own eyes. The need to fall in love and to have someone else fall in love with us does not require a particular person. The first step is having those basic needs met. Then the details of "personality meshing" can be filled in imaginatively. This personality meshing probably determines the future of the relationship established by a couple.

Couples who marry for healthy reasons and those who marry for unhealthy reasons have basically the same motivating forces propelling them toward marriage, but their intensity varies.

Most individuals are attracted toward one another by dependency needs. Every person has them, no matter how healthy they are. Healthy dependency needs reflect a desire to experience a sense of completion. When a person has exaggerated dependency needs, there is a desire for completion *and* for possession.

Self-esteem and its potential for enhancement propels people toward marriage. Everyone wants to receive affirmation of worth and value from the other person. Some have the excessive need for their spouses to make them feel worthy, good, attractive, wanted, desired, and so on. Gradually the excessive need can exact a strain upon the relationship.

The normal desire for affirmation, however, is also a strong attracting and maintaining force of marriage. The desire of increased self-esteem and dependency needs both build commitment, which has been called the glue of marriage. That glue is in the process of setting when a couple arrives for premarital instruction.

It is important to carefully assess the amount of dependency needs and need for self-esteem of each person during the process of the counseling. Asking the man and woman about the extent of each of those in their desire to marry has been both helpful and revealing with a number of couples.

Questions such as, In what way do you see yourself dependent upon your partner? and, How are you expecting your future spouse to enhance your self-esteem? have been helpful.

Marriage and mate selection is not a matter of chance. Mate selection is very purposeful, and people choose the persons they need at that point in time. On a conscious and subconscious level people do know what they are getting when they marry.

In their research of hundreds of couples Robert F. Stahmann and William J. Hiebert state:

> Our assumption that marriage is neither accidental nor dichotomous has been influenced by our clinical practice with the hundreds of couples we have seen both in marital counseling and in premarital counseling. In thinking about these couples and the manner in which they chose each other, we have discovered that the couples were apparently performing a task and involved in a process. It has struck us that many couples were involved in the task of finding some way to initiate growth. The growth could be in many areas. Perhaps it was in becoming more outgoing, more self-confident, more intimate, or some other dimension of their personality that they felt needed expansion. The mate they chose, therefore, from the millions of individuals available was exactly the person who could provide them with the kind of growth they needed. Some women, for example, seek out a particular man who can teach them to be tough, just as some men seek out a woman who can teach them to be soft. It almost seems to us that couples in some way find each other and choose each other on the basis of their potential to induce change. It is as if couples are in a strange way performing the task of therapy. Perhaps we could say that marriage is an amateur attempt at psychotherapy.
>
> All of this is a way of saying that we believe that marriage is purposeful and that couples choose each other on the basis of the ability of the other person to help them initiate growth. We think that couples are involved in a task of healing. It is as if many individuals at the point of dating and moving to marriage find themselves to be incomplete in some way. Their search for a mate is not haphazard but rather based on some kind of deeply intuitive homing device that relentlessly and purposely pursues exactly the kind of person who will provide them with the stimulation for the growth they are seeking. It is amazing how powerful that homing device can be.*[7]

Further complicating the matter of mate selection is the factor of the cultural "ideal mate" image, depending upon what marriage

*Reprinted by permission of the publisher from *Premarital Counseling* by Robert F. Stahmann and William J. Hiebert (Lexington, Mass.: Lexington Books, D.C. Heath and Company, Copyright 1980, D.C. Heath and Company).

means in a particular society. If, for example, marriage is primarily a division of labor and childrearing, the ideal wife would be one who is physically strong with broad shoulders and broad hips. Descriptions of masculine and feminine characteristics provided by a culture influence the ideal mate images. In one society the ideal woman is sweet and delicate, in another she is extroverted and sexually provocative. Culture defines it; we fit into the pattern.

Cultural definitions of the ideal mate can influence mate selection in two ways. Because this definition identifies what is desirable in a mate, it almost labels the desirability of each person. The closer a person gets to this cultural ideal, the more attractive he or she becomes to a greater number of people. And if the person realizes that he is approaching the ideal, he can be more selective in his own choice of a mate and hold out for the one closest to the ideal.

The second way in which this cultural definition of the ideal mate can influence mate selection is called "idealization of the mate." It means that, even if your choice does not meet the cultural standard of idealization, you attribute those characteristics to the person with whom you have fallen in love.

The choice of the partner is complicated by this human penchant for wishful thinking. Unfortunately, the more insecure a person is, the greater is his need for idealizing his partner.

Most people do not think about mate selection in a logical, analytical manner, but we are unconsciously influenced by these factors and in subtle ways we probably do adhere to them. Yet many people would vehemently deny these ideas, protesting that "it is our love that brought us together."

If cultural images influence one's selection of a mate, what about the images that parents have of their offspring's future mate? Parents exert considerable indirect control over the associations of their children; this in turn limits the field of possibilities for mate selection. College students feel this pressure less than those who remain at home. Parents help determine an acceptable grouping of eligibles from which their child may choose a mate.[8] Interestingly enough, when a woman's parents disapproved of her relationship with a young man (according to a study by Burgess and Wallin), more than twice as many relationships ended in broken engagements or early divorce as when both parents approved. The approval of the man's parents does not seem to be nearly as important.[9]

An interesting theory of who marries whom and why has been suggested by Bert Adams in "Mate Selection in the United States: A Theoretical Summarization." He describes mate choice as a process and isolates a series of factors that are involved.

It is more likely that individuals will marry if the following occurs:

(1) A person is dating someone who is near and available in time and space rather than a person who is not. An effect of proximity then is that there is a greater likelihood that one would meet, be attracted to, and marry someone of the same social category as him/herself. Proximity then puts a limiting condition on the number of eligible partners available for marriage.

(2) Physical attractiveness and similar interests also assist in early attraction.

(3) Early attraction is perpetuated and reinforced by favorable reaction by other significant people. If that does not come, the relationship may be weakened.

(4) Self-disclosure is another necessary ingredient so that rapport can develop. It is a matter of learning to feel comfortable in one another's presence.

If the conditions of favorable response and rapport are established, then deeper attraction can develop.

(5) Deeper attraction will continue to occur now if:

The couple's values are similar.

There is a similarity in physical attractiveness.

There is a personality similarity.

There are a number of barriers that need to be overcome before continuation of the relationship occurs. They include the area of differences such as race or religion. They will be significant *if* those differences matter to the couple. Another barrier is the negative reaction of significant others, especially if those are parents.

(6) An additional factor that can intrude into the development of the relationship is an alternate attraction. That is not limited to another person but could be education, involvement at work, a job change, a new hobby, and so on. The stronger the attraction, the more possible the current relationship could be terminated.

(7) It is at this point that the relationship moves even deeper. The reasons for that can be either healthy or unhealthy. For example, a person with low self-esteem tends to hang onto a relationship rather than run the risk of developing a new relationship.

(8) Other factors that propel the relationship forward are:

If the person sees the other as "the right one" or "the best I can get"

If the couple begin to be identified as a couple or are thought of as a couple

If one's identity is involved with the other person

All of this sounds very unromantic. Yet the courtship process does involve various stages whether the couple are consciously aware of them or not.[10]

After all is said and done, however, most people still come back to "we married because we loved one another." So what constitutes love? Many of the elements involved in mate selection discussed earlier are behind what we call love. But the emotional element of love lingers with us. Earlier the description of one romanticist was given: "Love is a feeling you feel when you feel that you're going to get a feeling that you never felt before." This is about the only way some people know how to describe their relationship.

What does all this have to do with the pastor and premarital counseling? It has everything to do with the potential success of the marriage relationship. If the pastor is the one conducting the premarital counseling, all the previously mentioned information should be etched upon his mind as he evaluates the motivation for a marriage. One should look for apparent and not-so-apparent reasons for marriage. Through skillful questioning, some of those before-mentioned factors may emerge. It is important to remember that the courtship and engagement period can be a deceptive time when fogged by romance.

Just where does the will of God enter into all this? How does one determine God's will for a mate?

Many people seem to rely upon inner impressions or feelings. Others say that the Lord revealed to them what they should do, and yet they are a bit fuzzy as to the means of this revelation. Many have the leading or impression that they should marry a certain person. What principles could a person follow? Dr. James Dobson has suggested four basic principles that a person may follow in knowing God's will for any area of his or her life. Those principles should be applied to any impressions that a person might have regarding marriage.

Is the impression scriptural? Guidance from God is always in accordance with His Word. If a Christian is considering marrying a non-Christian, there is no use in praying for God's will; the Scripture is clear concerning this situation. In searching the Scripture, verses should be taken within context, not in a random sampling.

Is the impression right? The expression of God's will should conform to God's universal principles of morality and decency. If human worth is depreciated or the integrity of the family is undermined by some "special leading," then it is probably not a leading from God.

Is it providential? Every impression ought to be considered in the light of providential circumstances. Are necessary doors opening or closing? Is God speaking through events?

Is the impression reasonable? Does the impression make sense? Is it consistent with the character of God to require it?"[11]

If a person has numerous mixed feelings about marrying the other individual, if there is no peace over the upcoming event, and if the majority of friends and relatives are opposed to the wedding, the decision ought to be reconsidered.

MARRIAGEABILITY TRAITS

Since most people eventually get married, it is important to be aware of the traits that make an individual a better partner and give him or her more potential to make a marriage work. There are eight basic factors that have been called marriageability traits: adaptability and flexibility, empathy, ability to work through problems, ability to give and receive love, emotional stability, similar family backgrounds, similarities between the couple themselves, and communication. If those elements are present, there is a greater likelihood of marital satisfaction and stability. As the counseling proceeds, one should be evaluating the couple in light of those factors.

Perhaps all these factors could be considered as some of the elements of compatibility. Many couples ask, "Are we compatible?" Compatibility can mean how well the intrinsic characteristics of two people *fit*. Compatibility between individuals can also determine how easily a relationship can be established. However, this provides only the potential for a good marriage; it is necessary, but not sufficient. The more compatible the better, but the potential must be activated and used. Compatibility is a matter of becoming and developing as well as being. No two people are ever entirely compatible.

Adaptability and *flexibility* are necessary ingredients. This means the person must be able to adjust to change with a minimum of rigidity. He must be able to accept the differences in his partner, adapt, and work toward a different life-style if necessary.

Charles Shedd, in his book *Letters to Philip*, tells the story of two rivers flowing smoothly and quietly along until they came together and joined. When this happened, they clashed and hurled themselves at one another. But as the newly formed river flowed downstream, it gradually quieted down and flowed smoothly again. Now it was broader and more majestic and had much more power. Dr. Shedd suggested that a good marriage is often like that. When two independent streams of existence come together, there will probably be some dashing of life against life at the junction. Personalities rush against one another, preferences clash, ideas contend for power, and habits vie for position. Sometimes, like the waves, they throw up a spray that leaves you breathless and makes you wonder where the loveliness has gone. But that's all right. Like the two rivers, what comes out of this struggle may be something deeper, more powerful than each river was on its own. This is what occurs in the adaptability process. Ephesians 4:2 says, "Because we love one another, we are willing to make allowances for one another" (Amp.).† It is vital that one learn to look at the interests of the other person, to consider the other's needs and ideas, and, because of love, to be willing to allow the other to think and do things differently. It means that a person evaluates his or her spouse's differences as being only differences—not marks of inferiority.

† *Amplified New Testament.*

Empathy is a positive characteristic necessary for all interpersonal relationships, and especially for those who are married. It is the ability to be sensitive to the needs, hurts, and desires of others, feeling with them and experiencing their world from their perspective. If they hurt, we hurt. If they are excited, we can be excited with them and understand and perceive their feeling response. Romans 12:15 tells us that we are to rejoice with those that rejoice and to weep with those that weep. This passage from the Word of God seems to reflect the idea of empathy.

Dr. Judson Landis, one of the foremost family sociologists, has said that the most marriageable people are those whose ability to empathize is high. They are able to use their empathetic ability in a very positive manner. They can control their words and actions so they do not say the wrong things that hurt the other individual.

A third marriagebility trait is the *ability to work through problems*. Problems, conflicts, and differences are part and parcel of marriage. Some couples run from and ignore problems, or give each other the silent treatment. Couples who accept and properly dispel and control their emotional reactions and clarify and define their problems and work together toward solutions, will in all likelihood remain married.

The *ability to give and receive love* is a trait that needs both elements for success. The giving of love involves more than just verbalizing it. It must also be evident in tangible ways that are identifiable and recognizable to both parties. Behavior, actions, and attitudes convey this in a meaningful manner. But just as important is the ability to accept love from another. Some people have such a need to be needed that they feel fulfilled by giving. To receive and accept love threatens them and lowers their sense of self-worth. If this nonacceptance response is continued, usually the other partner will give up or find someone else who will accept his love.

Emotional stability—accepting one's emotions and controlling them—lends balance to a relationship. We depend upon a person who has a consistent, dependable emotional response. Extreme flare-ups and decisions based upon emotional responses do not lend themselves to stable relationships.

The *more similar the family backgrounds*, the more contributions each can make to the marriage relationship. The greater the differences—economic, cultural, religious, being an only child compared to having several siblings, permanent living quarters compared to a high mobility rate—the more adjustments must be made. Those adjustments can add even more pressures to learning to live together. Naturally, the more mature the couple, the more easily the adjustments can be made.

Another trait, closely tied to similarity in family background, is *similarities between the couple themselves*. Earlier it was mentioned that like tends to marry like more than the opposite. If a couple has similar interests, likes and dislikes, friends, educational level, and religion, the marriage relationship is greatly enhanced.

The final trait that is necessary for a love relationship to develop is *communication*. There are differences in ability, styles, and beliefs about communication. Free interchange of ideas is essential. Communication is the ability to share in such a way that the other person can understand and accept what is being said. But listening is also involved. True listening means not thinking about what you are going to say when the other person stops talking. It means not making value judgments as to how the other person expressed himself and the words he used. It means that if you are really listening you can reflect back both the meaning and feeling of what was expressed. The tendency in our culture is for men not to communicate on a feeling response level, to verbalize less, and to be more solution-oriented instead of talking about the problem. This puts a great strain upon the marriage relationship.

Numerous studies made over the past two decades provide additional indicators of marital success which cannot be discounted. It appears to be a trait of human nature for those who differ radically from the norm in these characteristics to believe that they will be the exceptions and will make their marriage work in spite of gross differences. For a few it may work.

Various studies point out the importance of significant relationships with other people. If a person has experienced warm and satisfying relationships with both his father and mother, his marriage will be influenced positively. If the parents were affectionate, firm, consistent, and fairly well adjusted in their own marriage, this contributes to the new marriage relationship. Another interesting factor centers on friends of both sexes: if each person has friends, and these become and remain mutual friends after marriage, the marriage relationship will be enhanced.

Environmental conditions in the person's background, both social and physical, can influence the marriage somewhat. A happy childhood, lack of poverty, and completion of extensive formal education can contribute to success in marriage.

The socioeconomic level of a man's parents seems to affect the economic status of his own marriage. Research has indicated that stability and adjustment of the marriage are directly related to the income of the husband. The lower the husband's income, the greater the possibility that the marriage will be more unstable and maladjusted.

Another factor affecting marital success centers on particular events in the person's past and the timing of those events. Marriage at an early age is not favorable to a healthy adjustment nor to marital longevity. A brief whirlwind romance or a premarital pregnancy is an additional adverse condition. A good work record, definite and reasonable occupational plans, and a low residence-mobility factor contribute positively.

The most difficult factors to measure are the psychological attributes of the individuals. Yet they are important. A strong interest in family life, just as strong a commitment to make it succeed, and a willingness to work together are the positive points. Even if one person within a relationship will exert effort there is more chance of that marriage succeeding than if both just coast along.[12]

In past research there was some indication that for marital satisfaction to occur the wife must be able to understand and adapt to her husband. It seemed less important for the husband to understand his wife. But with the current emphasis upon greater equality within marriage, these findings should change.[13]

Couples who have reported happy marriages appear to concentrate their energy on their relationship. Those who seem less happy concentrate on situational aspects of marriage such as home, children, and social life as sources of their marital happiness. Feelings of happiness in marriage have a direct correlation to the way the partners are relating to one another.

Other studies reveal that in the area of communication happily married couples differ from unhappily married couples in the following ways: They (1) talk more to each other; (2) convey the feeling that they understand what is being said to them; (3) have a wider range of subjects available to them to discuss; (4) preserve their communication channels and work on keeping them open; (5) show more sensitivity to each other's feelings; (6) personalize their language symbols; and (7) make more use of additional nonverbal techniques of communication.[14]

One final element that must be present for any possibility of success is commitment. Robert Blood has summarized it best:

> Commitment is dangerous. It can be exploited. If my wife takes my commitment for granted, she may rest too easily on her laurels. Perhaps commitment should be not simply to each other as we are but to the highest potentialities we can achieve together. Commitment then would be to marriage not simply as a status but as a dynamic process. Let me commit myself to a lifelong adventure, the adventure of living with this woman. The route of this adventure has been only dimly charted by those who have gone before. Because I am unique and my partner is unique, our marriage will also be unique. We commit ourselves to undertaking this adventure together, and to following wherever it may lead. Part of the excitement of marriage is not knowing in advance what either the joys or the sorrows will be. We can be sure, however, that we will be confronted with countless challenges. Commitment provides the momentum for going forward in the face of those challenges.[15]

All these facts, then, should be part of the pastor's filtering system as he works with the couple. The counseling session will give him an opportunity to determine the potential qualities of the future relationship as well as family and individual differences.

NOTES

1. David Knox, *Marriage: Who? When? Why?* (Englewood Cliffs, N.J.: Prentice-Hall, Inc., 1974).
2. Ibid., pp. 136-42, adapted.
3. Lyle B. Gangsei, ed., *Manual for Group Premarital Counseling* (New York: Association, 1971), pp. 56-57.
4. J. Richard Udry, *The Social Context of Marriage*, 3d ed. (New York: Lippincott, 1974), p. 157, adapted.
5. Ibid., p. 157, adapted.
6. Robert Blood, Jr., *Marriage* (New York: Free Press, 1969), pp. 38-43, adapted.
7. Robert F. Stahmann and William J. Hiebert, *Pre-Marital Counseling* (Lexington, Mass.: Lexington Books, 1980), p. 18.
8. Udry, p. 187, adapted.
9. Ibid.
10. Excerpted from Bert Adams in *Contemporary Theories About the Family*, Wesley Burr, Reuben Hill, F. Ivan Nye, and Ira Reiss, eds. (New York: Free Press, n.d.), 1:259-67.
11. James Dobson, *Dr. James Dobson Talks About God's Will* (Glendale, Calif.: Gospel Light, Regal, 1974), pp. 13-21, adapted.
12. Udry, p. 236, adapted.
13. Leonard Benson, *The Family Bond—Marriage, Love and Sex in America* (New York: Random House, 1971), pp. 144-45, adapted.
14. Carlfred B. Broderick, ed., *A Decade of Family Research and Action* (Minneapolis: National Council on Family Relations, 1972), p. 66, adapted.
15. Blood, pp. 10-11.

3

Premarital Preparation and Enrichment— Purpose, Results, and Various Styles

At this point it should be apparent that there is an urgent need for premarital preparation. The local church or those who have some type of Christian ministry are in the best position to provide such a service. It is interesting and sad to note how lax the local church has been in having an ongoing, intensive, and mandatory program of premarital counseling.

Most people, layman and professional alike, believe that premarital counseling is a worthy concept. (The term *premarital preparation and enrichment* is a truer description of this process.)

Traditionally there have been three main groups that provide most of the premarital counseling: ministers, physicians, and professional mental health workers.

The first mention of premarital counseling as a valued service occurred in a 1928 article in *The American Journal of Obstetrics and Gynecology*. Then and until the mid-1950s, most of the writing concerned physicians and the premarital physical exam. In the fifties religious literature began to focus upon premarital counseling as well as writings from the mental health profession.

Several states have taken steps to stem the number of divorces that occur in youthful marriages. California and other states have passed legislation requiring persons under eighteen to obtain not only parental consent but also a court order giving permission to obtain the marriage license.

The Superior Court of Los Angeles County, along with courts in many other counties, mandated premarital counseling as a prerequisite for obtaining a marriage license by minors. Many churches and public health agencies offer their services to young couples seeking permission to marry. In 1972, of the 4,000 couples who applied for marriage licenses and needed court orders, 2,745 turned to ministers for their counseling. Many of the other couples used community health services. Even though the law and the program are just a few years old, initial findings have indicated the following conclusions concerning those couples involved in premarital counseling provided by public health services: couples used the information given to them as well as the resources of the public health program and many returned for counseling after marriage. The findings reinforced the conviction that premarital counseling is a valuable means of offering primary prevention about common problems, responsibilities, and satisfactions of marriage.[1]

What is the purpose of premarital counseling? What does the pastor or other counselor hope to accomplish by spending several hours with a couple? There are several goals for Christian premarital counseling. In the following discussion, these goals are not listed in order of importance.

One of the goals of the counseling is to make arrangements for the procedural details of the wedding ceremony itself. The couple can express their desires and the pastor can make suggestions and provide guidelines. Tremendous variation is found in wedding invitations and ceremonies today. A pastor should be flexible in his approach to the ceremony. Christian couples are becoming more vocal and personal in sharing their faith in Jesus Christ through their invitations and ceremony, thus allowing both to serve as vehicles for testimony as well as commitment and celebration.

Premarital counseling is a choice of opportunity for the pastor or other counselor to build an in-depth relationship with the couple, which could lead to a continuing ministry in the future. The rapport established now will make it easier to be involved in the excitement of the couple's marriage in years ahead.

A vital goal is providing correction. Correction of faulty information concerning marriage relationships, the communication process, finances, in-laws, sex, and so on, will be a regular part of the counseling for most couples. In fact, the pastor may be one of the few individuals involved in the life of the couple who can provide this corrective. Unfortunately, some pastors believe that, at this point, couples are not open to assistance and their minds are made up or romantically blinded. To the contrary, if counseling is presented in the proper manner and the pastor is well prepared, couples will look forward to each session as a unique learning experience and value it highly. Many couples have suggested that the content of premarital counseling should be given to college students prior to mate selection and then again at premarital counseling.

Providing information is another goal and is congruous with the process of correction. Probably more teaching occurs in this type of counseling than in any other. Part of this teaching involves helping the couple to understand themselves and what each one brings to marriage, to discover their strengths and weaknesses, and to be realistic about the adjustments they must make to have a successful relationship.

One of the main purposes is to help the couple eliminate as many surprises as possible from the impending marriage. By eliminating those and helping them become more realistic about the future, marital conflict will be lessened. That is exactly what I share verbally with the couple. I also let them know that by doing this they will then have a greater opportunity to build and enrich their marriage in the way they are dreaming of at the present time. Too many couples today are committing marital suicide because of lack of preparation.

The counselor must have expertise in many areas, because the couple is looking to him or her as the conveyor of helpful information. This is an opportunity to provide an atmosphere in which the couple can relieve themselves of fears and anxieties concerning marriage and settle questions or doubts that they have. This may also be a time in which strained and severed relationships with parents and in-laws will be restored.

Counseling also provides an opportunity for Christian growth.

Anyone giving premarital counseling should use it to assist the individuals to develop spiritually and thus build a firmer basis for the marriage relationship. Couples should be given instruction in personal and family devotions before marriage. As they develop a pattern and grow in their marriages, these couples could eventually minister to other couples in the congregation.

The final purpose for counseling may seem foreign to some and yet could be one of the most important goals. This is a time to assist the couple in making their final decision, Should we marry? They may not come with that in mind, but engagement is not finality. Research indicates that between 35 and 45 percent of all engagements in this country are terminated. Many people do change their mind. Perhaps during the process of premarital counseling, some couples will decide to postpone their wedding or completely terminate their relationship. On the other side, there will be some cases in which the pastor will decide that he cannot, in good conscience, perform the wedding because of the apparent mismatch or immaturity of the couple. Some couples will listen to his advice; others will simply go elsewhere and find someone who does not require so much and will perform the ceremony.

Couples will change their minds. During the spring of one year I worked with nine different couples in premarital counseling, spending six sessions with each couple. Six of the couples proceeded with their weddings, and three chose not to proceed. One of the latter decided two weeks before the ceremony. Two couples had such a poor relationship that I planned to tell them their marriages would be too much of a risk; before I did, they told me they had decided to break off their relationships.

What are the results of this program of counseling, and are they significant? Very little has been done in terms of extensive research and statistical studies with a long-range approach. Two research reports will be cited, as well as individual responses. A Baptist pastor in Oregon made his own follow-up study of couples who had completed his five sessions of premarital counseling. In 1973 he stated that he had performed between 170 and 180 weddings since 1958. He followed up on those couples and learned that six had divorced. He also had refused to marry a number of couples because he felt their marriages would be too risky. (Remaining married is not always an indication of success;

many tolerate unhappy and unfulfilling marriages for years.)

Lt. Col. John Williams, a faculty member of the United States Air Force Academy in Colorado Springs, reported in his doctoral thesis that divorce among US military officers is significantly lower than among the population as a whole. Among military officers, air force officers were found to have the lowest divorce rate, with the lowest of all found among officers graduating from the Air Force Academy. Between the years of 1959, when the first class graduated, and 1970, only 21 of the 4,500 Air Force Academy graduates (.004 percent) were divorced.

Those statistics may be explained in part by the high value placed on stable marriage. A premarital counseling program conducted by the chaplaincy is an indication of the importance of successful marriage to the air force. Cadets and their fiancées are given intensive preparation for marriage which takes place after graduation from the academy. Protestant, Catholic, and Jewish chaplains conduct their own programs.

Catholic chaplains spend eight to fourteen hours counseling each couple, covering basic areas of communication, finances, love, responsible child planning, and in-laws. The final preparation is accomplished at a weekend retreat where marriage counselors, gynecologists, and lawyers share their views and experiences with the couples.

The Protestant program includes seminars on Sunday afternoons in January, February, and March. The subjects discussed include the success rate of air force marriages, methods of communication, and the physical and spiritual aspects of marriage. A marriage retreat is conducted in April.[2]

In the winter of 1976 a research study was conducted concerning the types, extent, and results of premarital counseling done in churches. Over one thousand churches were contacted, and four hundred seven returned usable surveys. Over twenty-five different denominations were represented, with churches ranging in size from thirty people to over six thousand people. Some important results are: The average number of sessions required for premarital counseling was three. Forty-five pastors required only one session, and forty-four required at least six sessions. Two hundred seventy-four stated that they performed weddings for nonbelievers; sixty-nine reported they did not. Three hundred sixty-nine indicated that premarital counseling was required, and thirty-eight stated that it was not. Three of the most significant questions asked the participants were:

1. What are the four most significant questions that you ask the couples during the counseling? The results of this question were very helpful, but space does not allow a complete presentation of this information. (A complete report of this study is available, including these questions, from Christian Marriage Enrichment, 1913 E. 17th St., Suite 118, Santa Ana, CA 92701.

2. If counseling is mandatory, how do couples react? How does the church respond to this? Over 90 percent of the responses to this question were positive. People were in favor of the policy, felt that it helped, and encouraged their friends to come for counseling. Some couples were hesitant or went elsewhere.

3. What are the results of premarital counseling in your experience, and how do you know?

A representative sampling of responses is as follows:

- Very good: based upon the couples' feedback and the strength of their marriages.

- Several have postponed or canceled weddings.

- It has opened up couples to marital counseling that they otherwise would not have had.

- About 20 percent do not marry. They cancel their arrangements.

- Some couples decide that they are not ready for marriage. Some have come to know Christ as Savior.

- Many have expressed gratitude. Only two have been divorced (about 70 marriages in 22 years).

- Most couples have appreciated the sessions.

- Twenty-five percent of couples from one church decided not to get married. Almost another 25 percent have postponed their wedding dates. Many couples have been very outspoken in their appreciation and in encouraging friends to take the course.

- One pastor counseled fifty-seven couples and conducted weddings for twenty-three. Out of the first eleven he married before he learned how to conduct premarital counseling, one couple divorced and five couples are still having real struggles. After training, he counseled forty-five couples. They now have proper ground rules for their marriages and even for disagreeing and are developing successful marriages.

In 1978-79 an extensive marriage and family survey was conducted throughout the United States upon a Christian population. Over eight thousand took part in that survey with more than twenty-five denominations represented. Of the 109 questions, several were focused upon premarital preparation.

Questions and responses included the following: Prior to your own marriage did you receive premarital counseling from the church or pastor where you were married?

Three thousand forty-four stated yes, and 4,921 said no. An additional 571 said they received premarital counseling from a professional counselor. A total of 45 percent of those participating in the survey received some preparation.

The number of sessions couples received varied greatly with varying responses and results.

Number of Sessions	Percent That Attended
1	45
2	18
3	14
4	7.5
5	4
6	4
7 +	4

A very significant question was: "If you did receive premarital counseling, do you feel that it helped you in your marriage?"

Definitely Yes—29.3 percent
Possibly Yes —45.5 percent
Possibly No   —13.2 percent
Definitely No —11.2 percent

Only 15 percent of those who participated in one session stated that it definitely helped their marriage, and 31 percent of those who received two sessions of counseling said it definitely helped. It was significant that of those who received five sessions, 53 percent said that counseling definitely helped their marriage and of those who received seven or more sessions, 75 percent stated that premarital counseling definitely helped their marriage.

A statistical study and analysis was done upon the effect of premarital counseling as seen by responses to other questions. Some of the facts derived from this research indicate the following:

- More of those who received premarital counseling say they entered marriage with an adequate understanding of what it would be like, than those who did not receive counseling.
- More respondents who received premarital counseling describe their marriage as fulfilled and continuing than do the respondents who did not receive counseling.
- More of those who received premarital counseling strongly believe that knowing and having a personal relationship with Jesus Christ has made a positive difference or has had positive effect on their marriage than those who did not receive premarital counseling.
- More of those who received premarital counseling believe that the teachings and application of Scripture have helped their marriage relationship in a positive manner, than those who did not receive premarital counseling.
- Among those who received premarital counseling the major responsibility for disciplining the children is equally shared more often than among those who did not receive premarital counseling.
- Fewer respondents who had received premarital counseling listed communication in the top four areas in which they would like the most additional help, than those who had not received premarital counseling.
- Fewer respondents who received premarital counseling listed how to resolve conflicts in the top four areas in which they would like the most additional help than those who had not received premarital counseling.

The basic structure of the premarital counseling suggested in this book is six one-hour sessions before the wedding plus one session three to six months after the wedding. Your initial reaction might be, "How do we fill all of that time?" The problem is actually just the opposite—sometimes the time allotted is not sufficient to cover all the material. (I find now that I often take at least seven sessions as a minimum.)

Other readers might react by saying, "I marry twenty to thirty couples a year. What you're suggesting could amount to two-hundred hours. Where do I get that time, with everything else that I have to do?" It is true that counseling takes time. However, it might be well for each minister to regularly analyze what he is doing with his time. Are his gifts and abilities being used to their best advantage? It is all too easy in the ministry to become overwhelmed with tasks that have little to do with a real ministry to people. Often it comes down to a matter of priority; we do what we feel is important. Premarital counseling is one of the most important opportunities for ministry.

There are several ways to approach the problem of time. One is to restructure one's use of time so that counseling takes a higher priority and other activities are delegated. When we keep adding ministries to our already busy schedule and fail to relinquish or delegate some, a number of difficulties arise. (See Exod. 18 and Num. 11; note the difficulty Moses experienced because he had not delegated responsibilities to others.)

If the church has a multiple staff, several or all of the ministers could conduct the premarital counseling. A number of churches have trained lay couples to do portions of the counseling, thus using the gifts of many as well as helping the pastoral staff.

Another approach is to conduct some or all of the premarital counseling in group sessions. Examples of this will be given later in the chapter.

It is important to educate the congregation concerning the pastor's policy of premarital counseling—a task that could take a full year. Through the pulpit, classes, the church newsletter, and the bulletin, the pastoral staff has the opportunity to educate the congregation concerning the importance of marriage and the family and to describe in detail what is covered in premarital counseling. People in many congregations have expressed the wish that premarital counseling had been available to them years before.

On the other hand, some will resent a mandatory program and will threaten to go elsewhere for their wedding and perhaps even find another church home. That is their choice. If they so decide, the pastor should not allow himself to be manipulated and pressured into lowering his standards. Too often it has been too easy to be married within the local church. A couple must be willing to take time to adequately prepare for marriage. Through a consistent program such as this, the community and the people in the congregation will come to a deeper level of respect for the ministry of the church.

It is also true that a pastor may have fewer weddings under his new policy. But those he does have will be significant. The Reverend Robert Dulin, Jr., expressed this standard in his excellent address at the Congress on the Family in 1975 when he said, "Pastors should refuse to sell the birthright of their ministry to nurture marriages, for the pottage of conducting a wedding. The church's ministry is not to conduct weddings. Its ministry is to nurture marriages, before marriage and during marriage. If couples cannot make a commitment to nurture their marriage prior to the event, then the church should say we cannot have your marriage solemnized here."

There may be board members or relatives of members of the church who will ask for a special dispensation in the case of their own young person. A son who is home on leave from the army for a week wants to get married; a couple where there is a pregnancy wants a quick and quiet wedding. Many other unique circumstances will arise. Couples involved in these situations are usually in even greater need of counseling and preparation than the ordinary couple, and they too should complete the total program of premarital counseling.

Part of the process of educating the congregation will be to give periodic reminders about the steps involved in scheduling a wedding at the church. Couples should consider starting their counseling at the time of engagement, or in some cases, prior to engagement. It is best to conduct the counseling no later than four to six months before the wedding. There are two reasons for this. One is that the counseling lasts six to eight weeks, since the sessions are a week or ten days apart.

The second reason for starting counseling early is that the wedding date is not put on the church calendar when the couple first calls the church. The pastor waits until he feels that he favors the marriage and that he can conduct the wedding; at that point the couple can go ahead and set the date on the church calendar. That may occur after two sessions, or, for some, after five. A couple may ask to have a date on the calendar held for them, with the clear understanding that this does not constitute setting the date officially.

Undertaking the counseling does not automatically insure the couple that the wedding will be performed. The pastor will have several criteria to use in making this determination. (They will be discussed later.) With that approach, couples will soon learn to make their plans well in advance. That has advantages for the entire church.

If several churches in a community would adopt this approach, couples would soon begin to see how deeply the church values the marriage relationship and how important the preparation is. At a large church in southern California, a couple asked to see one of the pastors on the staff. When the pastor said that he would require five to six sessions of counseling, the couple said they did not want to have that much counseling and would ask one of the other staff members to perform the ceremony. When they arrived for their appointment with the next minister, they were surprised to hear he had the same requirement. They tried a third minister on the staff, and when they heard the same approach, they returned to the first one and said, "If so many of you on this staff believe so much in premarital counseling and its value, we've decided that we ought to have it. We'd like you to put us through the counseling."

Another way of providing the premarital counseling is through a group preparation program. A Catholic priest in Dodge City, Kansas, reports a program of premarital counseling in which lay couples had been trained to conduct the sessions. Forty couples were spread throughout the area and took two or three engaged couples at a time into their homes and provided several sessions of premarital counseling.

Grace Community Church in Panorama City, California, has a large number of couples married each year. To adequately provide for premarital counseling, a class session is conducted on Sunday mornings. Each couple must attend at least five sessions in order to be married at the church. Some of the couples receive individual sessions as well, based upon the results of their personality tests. Between twenty and thirty couples take this course. Listed here is the outline.

Session	Topics
1	Purpose of Course
	Purpose of Engagement
	Outline of Course

2	T-JTA (Taylor-Johnson Temperament Analysis) Test Results Returned	
3	Communication	
4	Health	Family Background
	Education	Employment
	Housing	Leisure Time
5	In-laws	Children
	Finances	Sexual Adjustment

Weekly homework assignments assist the individuals, as persons and as a couple, to think through and evaluate their beliefs, values, and goals. The assignments also enable those counseling to better evaluate the strengths and potential weaknesses of the couples in order to be of greater assistance to them. The "contact couple" assigned (explained below) are the only individuals other than the teaching staff who ever see the work turned in. Homework is handed in on a weekly basis because the assignments are coordinated with the subjects discussed at the next session.

Contact couples are carefully selected married couples who are asked to work on a one-to-one basis with an engaged couple in the course. Each engaged couple is afforded the opportunity to receive personal counsel, interaction, and exposure to a Christian married couple within the latter's own home setting. Homework assignments or any other topic may be discussed. The time spent is left to the discretion of the contact couple.

Optional discussion and fellowship studies are held on selected Friday evenings during the course. The studies are designed to provide additional input, interaction, and fellowship. Topics of practical importance for a mature marriage relationship are covered. Selected couples from Grace Church are invited to lead the discussions.

A resource library of excellent books and tapes is provided for those involved in the course.

Questions that most pastors ask are, What standard do we use in evaluating whom we marry and whom we don't? Do we marry just Christians, or do we become involved with non-Christians? What about those who have been divorced? What should be done there?

A pastor will have two Christians coming to be married, two non-Christians, and one Christian and one non-Christian. One cannot assume that just because two believers are involved the marriage should occur automatically. A Christian profession alone is not sufficient. And that is what the premarital counseling is all about—making that determination.

A basic standard that could be used with any couple is that if they are immature, have unrealistic expectations about marriage, have low motivation to complete the assignments during counseling, and cannot adapt or change, they should postpone the marriage. Some might be urged not to marry at all.

The material given in this book will help a counselor establish criteria for marrying or not marrying. Some of the questions to consider during evaluation are:

Are any legal requirements being violated, such as license, consent of parents for minors, health test, waiting period? Are any of your own church requirements being ignored?

Do these persons give frivolous reasons for wanting to get married?

Is one (or both) entering marriage under duress?

Are they so immature mentally and emotionally that they do not understand the meaning of the vows or give reasonable promise of fulfilling them?

Are their indications that they do not intend to fulfill their marriage vows?

Are there any serious mental, emotional, physical, or other handicaps that might endanger their marriage? Have those been adequately understood, accepted, and dealt with insofar as possible?

Is there such marked personality incompatibility that the need for psychological testing is indicated?

Are there differences in age, background, values, and so forth, that will enrich or threaten their relationship?

If this is a second marriage, has sufficient time elapsed since the death or divorce for the widowed or divorced person to have overcome the hurt and made adequate preparation for the new marriage?

Some pastors favor a preliminary brief session with the couple to discuss their spiritual life. Whether this is done prior to the onset of the actual premarital counseling or during the first session is up to the individual counselor. The details for this session are presented in the next chapter.

When it comes to a believer and an unbeliever's seeking marriage, the Scriptures clearly forbid the uniting of such a couple (see 2 Cor. 6:14); this would be the standard for refusing to perform the ceremony. As a couple comes for the interview where this information is shared, the pastor's response in love and concern and his high regard for the scriptural teaching could make an impression upon the unbeliever so that the door for discussion remains open. This is an opportunity for evangelism. Yet if one does make a response at this time it is important to spend time with the person to eliminate the possibility that it was a pseudoprofession designed to get the pastor to conduct the wedding.

It is very difficult to judge motives. The pastor dealing with a premarital conversation should engage the person in a thorough discussion of the meaning of a commitment to Christ. He should watch for external evidence that indicates a change of life.

If a person does respond to the claim of the gospel, he or she should be guided into a group that will assist him or her in the Christian life. In many such cases the wedding date, if it is relatively close at hand, might be postponed in order to let the new convert grow in the faith. That growth is especially important for men because of the biblical concept of the leadership role of the Christian husband. If both partners are at a similar level in their Christian walk it is easier for them to grow together and study together. In some instances the new convert may pass the other person in Christian development and become a source of spiritual encouragement.

A number of pastors in evangelical churches have stated that they do perform weddings joining believer and unbeliever. Their reasons include pressure from parents who are members, board-member pressure, fear of offending long-standing friends, and doubt that the non-Christian would respond to any proclamation at this time. A pastor may weigh in his mind what his congregation will think about what he does. His feeling of the approval or disapproval of the church figures in his decision. A common, final reason is that if the couple is allowed to marry, the unbeliever may eventually respond to the church and its message through this contact. Too often, though, the opposite occurs:

because of the influence of the one, both individuals are lost to the church, and the faith of the believer begins to wane. In most of these cases it is the woman who is the Christian, and the man who is not. As difficult as it may seem to some, the biblical standard must remain the guide for the church.

Wayne Oates has graphically summarized the church's position:

> Marriage under the auspices of the church is an institution ordained of God, blessed by Christ's presence, and subject to the instruction of the Holy Spirit. This is what is meant when a church says it will not "join any person together other than as God's Word doth allow." If there is any other standard, the church is consciously yoking two people together unequally. The Christian experience of regeneration is a necessary prerequisite for a congregation's participating in a Christian wedding through the ministry of its pastor. God has not promised that even a Christian marriage will be free of tribulation. However, when a church joins couples together apart from the Christian faith, it shares the responsibility for any future failure of the marriage for the very reason it did not communicate the redemptive transforming love of Christ at the time of the wedding.
>
> One very real objection can legitimately be raised here. Some people say that a pastor and a congregation can marry a couple, even if one or both may not be Christians, with the hope that by being kind at this point, by doing things they may want it to do, it will have an opportunity later to win them to Christ. However, being kind to people does not necessarily consist of doing what they want done. It may even be the deepest sort of unkindness. Furthermore, there is always suspicion of the wisdom of the man or woman who marries with an eye to "reforming" the mate. If this is true of the couple's individual relationship to each other, it certainly is true of the relationship of the pastor and the church to them. When a church offers the services of its pastor with a view to the couple's being changed at some later date, it forthwith misrepresents reality to the couple.[3]

Pastors are divided over the question of what to do for couples when both claim to be unbelievers. Such a couple seeks a church wedding not to reflect their commitment to Christ, but because of sentiment, status, or because the church represents the place to be married. Some pastors agree to perform this service for a couple, acting more as an agent of the state than as a minister of the gospel. The ceremony is usually held in the pastor's study and does not involve a regular church wedding. The content of this ceremony includes only what is necessary to fulfill the law. Yet it seems that this function could be performed by a justice of the peace. The pastor's time should be committed to bringing people to Christ and building strong, enriched marriages; time available for weddings should be reserved for believers.

A Christian wedding involves vows taken before God, scriptural teaching and references which pertain to Christians, a blessing and benediction from God upon the husband and wife, a time of testimony to their faith in Christ, a commitment to build their marriage upon biblical teachings, and a time of celebration and praise. It should also be a time when those who attend the celebration are asked to uphold the couple in prayer and encouragement. Is it possible that nonbelievers could honestly go through this type of ceremony? Could a pastor honestly lead them through it?

When unbelieving couples ask for a wedding, those reasons can be clearly and lovingly explained. The pastor could also suggest that they continue meeting to explore together the meaning of the Christian faith. Some will respond, but some will never return; they will seek a place where their request will be honored. If a couple remains and professes faith in Christ, then the process of Christian growth begins, and a wedding is a possibility in the future.

In an article entitled, "Church Weddings Are Not for Everyone," Pastor Grant Swank, Jr., shared his philosophy:

> I will not perform the wedding ceremony for persons who are not, both by profession and by practice, Christians. Because of this, I have been regarded by some as a strange sort of clerical animal, unkind at best, cruel at worst. Yet no matter what the reaction, my convictions are firm.
>
> How did I reach this position? Partly through the realization that a very large percentage of the marriages I had performed had ended in divorce! At the outset of my ministry, I married any couple who asked me to do so. I counseled them before the wedding. Courtesies were exchanged among all concerned. The manners were well polished both in the study and in the sanctuary. However, often something disastrous happened after all the hoopla died down. As time passed—in some cases only a brief

time—the vows and prayers of the ceremony were forgotten, and the marriage crumbled.

This happened time and time again among those who had little or no real spiritual commitment to begin with. I was pressed to the conclusion that I was wrong in officiating at a wedding of two unbelievers.

The more I thought about it, the more it seemed a charade. Was I called of God to perform marriages for people in the house of the Lord when those persons had not committed their lives to the Lord? Was I to say prayers for two people who did not pray? Was I to read passages from the Bible to a bride and groom knowing full well that they did not intend to build their home upon that Bible? Was I to ask these two people to utter their promises in the presence of Jesus when they did not regard Jesus as the Lord of their lives? Was I to conclude the ceremony by earnestly beseeching God's blessing upon their new life together when they were not founding that life on the rock of salvation? They gave the Almighty only a nod of attention day in and day out; but on their special day, I, the man of God, was to call forth heavenly beatitudes upon their future.

Enough of this, I decided. I was being used. God was being used. The church and the truths the church stood for were being used. What the couples wanted out of it all was the beauty of the sanctuary, the noble sound of the organ, the dignified image of the clergyman, the luxury and respectability of a "church wedding."

What if I allowed a person to be baptized, knowing full well that he did not profess Jesus as Saviour? What if I told the congregation that anyone could receive communion, whether or not he was committed to Christ? What if I accepted into church membership anyone, no matter what he thought about the doctrines of the body of Christ? I would be asked to leave my pulpit. The governing session of the congregation would not stand for a minister with such a loose regard for those things held sacred. Yet I could go on year after year performing weddings that apparently were little more than hollow recitations of time-honored words.

My conclusion jelled when I reread in a new light the plain words of Second Corinthians 6:14: "Do not be mismated with unbelievers. For what partnership have righteousness and iniquity? Or what fellowship has light with darkness?" (RSV).* I realized that I had been partner to "mismating." I had joined light

*Revised Standard Version.

with darkness. And I had more times than not joined darkness with darkness.

Now when I perform a wedding, it is a time for genuine rejoicing in the Spirit of God. All persons gathered in the sanctuary know that the two being brought together are dedicated to the Lord. What a glad time it is, and what a peaceful time for me, the officiating clergyman! My prayers are sent to God with a new sense of earnestness. The Scriptures are read to the worshipers with the knowledge that the bride and groom have grounded their lives upon the Book. The vows are taken with the understanding that God is entering as a third party into those promises. And my conscience is clear before all concerned. When the last amen is said in that ceremony, one can sense the spiritual excitement of those gathered in the house of prayer. I would never go back to the old practice of performing marriages only because I thought I was expected to do it as a part of my job.

Some fellow ministers ask if I am missing witnessing opportunities because of my policy. But I do have an opportunity to witness. When asked to marry a couple, I invite them to come for a talk. When we meet I confront them with the forgiveness and new life that Jesus offers, asking them if they will become disciples of the Lord. At that moment the encounter with God is established. If they respond negatively, then I kindly state that I can go no further, for my first obligation is to see that they are saved. If they refuse that salvation, then I cannot in good conscience proceed.

If they respond positively, then I congratulate them, pray for them, give them a Bible and Christian literature, tell them of the times of our church services, and invite them to attend. And I tell them that six months hence I will be glad to perform their wedding if they are still living daily for Christ, are active in the church, are spending time in prayer and Scripture reading.

The divorce rate keeps on increasing. One out of three marriages in the country ends in divorce (two out of three in California). But according to a study cited by Billy Graham, one out of forty marriages ends in divorce when parents attend church regularly, and only one out of four hundred ends in divorce when both parents with their children attend church regularly and maintain family devotions.

I have a feeling that I am on the right biblical track—for the good of the people, the good of sound doctrine, and the good of my own conscience. And the marriages performed since I adopted this policy will bear me out.[4]

It would be difficult to leave this section of the book without facing what some have called a dilemma. What are the guidelines to follow when faced with a couple of whom one or both have been married and divorced? One concern should be with the person's relationship to Christ and his or her Christian walk. Another concern should be with the previous relationship. The discussion should determine whether all past matters have been settled biblically.

There are many views today concerning divorce and remarriage. Some take the position that there is no biblical basis for divorce or for remarriage. However, it does appear from certain passages that divorce is permissible in some cases, and if so, remarriage would also seem to be accepted. (For a thorough discussion of divorce and remarriage, see *Divorce* by John Murray, Presbyterian & Reformed Publishing Co.; *Divorce and Remarriage* by Guy Duty, Bethany Fellowship, and *The Right to Remarry* by Dwight H. Small, Revell.)

It is difficult to obtain all the facts concerning the previous marriage situation, but the pastor ought to try to determine whether the divorce occurred according to biblical grounds: if there were attempts at reconciliation, if the divorced person is bitter or forgiving, and so on. If a person states that the spouse was the one at fault, the one who did the cheating, it is still important to ask, "Can you think of any way in which you might have had some responsibility in the demise of the first marriage?" or, "In what way do you feel that you contributed to the problems?" It is rare that only one person is at fault.

Other questions to ask are, What would you like to be different in this second marriage than it was in the first, and how will you make this difference? What did you learn from the first experience that will benefit you in this new relationship?

If one or both have children, spend time exploring their understanding of the process of child rearing from a biblical perspective. Philosophies of discipline usually conflict; the counselor can provide suggestions for handling the situation. (Materials for this purpose are suggested in a later chapter.)

As a pastor interviews a person or a couple considering marriage after divorce, the following questions should be considered:

What is the level of spiritual maturity of each individual? What is the evidence of the presence of Christ in their relationship?

Were those people Christians at the time of the divorce (one or both), or have they become Christians since the divorce? What effect has divorce had upon them in terms of their relationship to Christ?

What did the person(s) learn from the first experience? In what way are they the same or different since the divorce?

Has that person undergone some type of counseling or therapy during the first marriage or since that time? Are there any psychological or medical problems which need treatment before that person enters into the marriage? (That is where the testing portion of the premarital counseling program may help to uncover some problem areas.)

Is the couple capable of making a marriage work financially? The man's financial commitments to the first marriage may jeopardize the second. Finances undermine many marriages.

What do they see as the church's response to their marriage, and what are they seeking in terms of their future life in the local church?

Again Wayne Oates summarizes the church's position:

> If a couple have become faithful Christians and have demonstrated their change of heart and life since they have been divorced, a church will be hard put to refuse to marry them without placing its teaching concerning divorce above its doctrine of regeneration. Especially is this true if these people are deprived of a Christian wedding and at the same time awarded the privileges of church membership and of holding positions of leadership in the church. The wisdom of an earlier Episcopal ruling is still valid: a couple is required to wait at least one whole year after the date of the legal decree of divorce before remarriage. This ruling prevents a couple from "by-passing" the grief process of the previous marital break-up and from hastening into a premature relationship that may have been one precipitating cause of the previous marital collapse.[5]

NOTES

1. Helen Shonick, "Pre-Marital Counseling, Three Years' Experience of a Unique Service," *The Family Coordinator* (July 1975), p. 321.
2. *Religious News Service* (15 May 1974), p. 2.
3. Wayne Oates and Wade Rowatt, *Before You Marry Them* (Nashville: Broadman, 1975), p. 34. Used by permission.
4. J. Grant Swank, Jr., "Church Weddings Are Not for Everyone," *Christianity Today*, 27 August 1976, pp. 26-27. Copyright 1976 by *Christianity Today*. Used by permission.
5. Oates and Rowatt, pp. 38-39. Used by permission.

4

Resources to Use in Premarital Counseling

Earlier I suggested that a couple be required to have at least six sessions of premarital counseling. Here is how those sessions are organized. During the first session the pastor meets with both partners. Next he sees each one individually, each for one hour. It makes no difference whether the man or the woman is seen first. The sessions may occur during the same week or could be a week apart. The individual sessions are considered the second session. The third through the sixth sessions are held with the couple together. Sometimes additional individual sessions may be called for because of emotional difficulties discovered through testing. Following the sixth session, my wife, Joyce, and I have dinner with the couple.

The final and seventh session occurs six months after the wedding. It is called a marital evaluation and enrichment session. During that time I ask two questions of each of them that seem to be all that are needed to use the time effectively. They are, What are to be the most positive experiences you have had during the first six months of marriage? and, Where have you had the greatest difficulty during the past six months?

The setting where the counseling takes place is very important. The pastor's office or a study at home could be used if they have sufficient privacy and a homey, informal atmosphere. Freedom from interruptions is crucial; the pastor should make arrangements to prevent people from walking into the room, knocking on the door, and calling on the phone. When the pastor and the couple sit near each other in easy chairs, an informal setting is created that helps alleviate the couple's anxieties.

Part of the structure of this counseling and one of the requirements for the couple is that they must agree to complete the assignments given during the time of training. Several books, tapes, and tests are used in the assignments.

Many books could be used. Each pastor will probably have certain volumes which appeal to him. However, it is of value to be widely read in the area of marriage and family, as some books are more applicable for one couple than for another.

Many couples are assigned *No-Fault Marriage* by Marcia Lasswell and Norman M. Lobsenz (New York: Ballantine, 1977). That secular book has been very helpful and is one of the finest books written during the past decade. I ask each person to read one book that applies only to himself or herself. The woman is asked to read *Woman: Aware and Choosing* by Betty Coble, Broadman Press. Of the multitude of books written today for women, that work seems to have a balanced approach to the role of the wife without emphasizing a number of subtle manipulation techniques. The man is asked to read *What Wives Wish Their Husbands Knew About Women* by James Dobson, Tyndale. Reading that book prior to marriage should help a man avoid some common problems that occur.

Each partner is asked to read *Intended for Pleasure* by Dr. Ed and Gail Wheat, Revell. Reading that book and listening to the tape series mentioned later should give any couple a thorough understanding of the physical process. Those resources save hours of counseling time, as the pastor needs only to deal with any questions or reactions that arise from the input of these materials.

Communication—Key to Your Marriage is my own book, published by Regal. I ask couples to read a chapter, write their answers to the discussion questions, and discuss their responses. There will be times when the couple could spend hours in discussion; that is the very purpose of the premarital counseling program.

When the couple comes for the first session it is vital that they be told that they will probably spend thirty to thirty-five hours of work outside the sessions. They should look over their schedules and arrange time for study and discussion. That is another reason the actual counseling should take place well ahead of the wedding, for wedding preparations could take precedence over the counseling and its homework, which are more important.

The most essential book is *Before You Say I Do* by Wes Roberts and H. Norman Wright (Irvine, Cal.: Harvest, 1978). Each person needs a copy of that workbook, for it contains almost all the written assignments needed during the premarital sessions. The couple will be assigned specific chapters to work through and discuss each week. In a sense that material becomes a diary of the premarital experience. The couple is asked to review the workbook together on their first wedding anniversary. One of the financial and money management resources mentioned later in this book should also be assigned during the later sessions.

Many tape resources available today can be used to cover the roles of husband and wife. It would be advantageous if a pastor listened to the various sets and had them available to use with couples. The selection will depend upon what a couple has already listened to and upon the emphasis the pastor feels the couple needs.

I ask couples to listen to the tape series entitled *Enriching Your Marriage* by Wes Roberts and H. Norman Wright. That series covers the topics: The Purpose of Marriage, Love, Differences, Expectations, Goals, and Needs. An alternate series published by Christian Marriage Enrichment, containing four tapes, is entitled *The Pillar of Marriage—Communication.*

One of the finest sets of tapes available on sex was made by Dr. Ed Wheat, a Christian physician and surgeon, founder of The Bible Believer Cassette Ministry in Springdale, Arkansas. The series, titled *Sex Problems and Sex Techniques in Marriage,* has been of tremendous assistance to thousands of couples who have been married for many years as well as to those preparing for marriage. The couple is asked to listen to this series together a month or so before the wedding. Topics covered in this series include "The Command to Have Sexual Union," "Anatomy of the Male and Female Reproductive Systems," "Phases of Sexual

Response," "Sexual Problems," "Explanation of the Menstrual Cycle," "Birth Control," "Sex After 60-70-80," "Frequently Asked Questions and Answers About Sex," "The Greatest Enjoyment in the Sexual Union," and "The Purpose of the Sexual Union." For some reason, listening to a qualified doctor discuss the material frankly and openly has greater impact than reading the same words in print. One of the tapes concludes with a clear gospel presentation. All tape series are available from Christian Marriage Enrichment, 1913 E. 17th St., Suite 118, Santa Ana, CA 92701.

Later in the counseling the couple is asked to listen to the six tape series "Christian Financial Management" by Larry Burkett.

Tests and evaluation forms for premarital counseling provide valuable information and save time. One such test is the *Sex Knowledge Inventory,* from Family Life Publications, which has been used in that type of counseling to help a couple and their pastor determine the couple's level of knowledge and understanding of the basic physiology of the sexual response. However, the use of the book and the tapes by the Wheats should cover that subject adequately, and a pastor may not need the inventory.

From time to time one encounters an individual, usually a man, who feels that the book and tapes would be a waste of time as he considers himself quite knowledgeable in the field. Having him take the *Sex Knowledge Inventory* quickly dispels that belief and makes him more receptive to the instruction. Form Y of the test deals with such technical subjects as anatomy, physiology, and contraception. Form X may be more helpful in the counseling process as the questions are broader in scope and can also reflect some of the individual's attitudes. Several sample questions from form X are listed here.

What is the relation[ship] between being sexually attracted to a man or woman and being in love with that person?

A. Sex attraction is physical desire; love is an attitude.
B. Sex attraction and being in love are the same thing.
C. If there is no sex attraction, there can be no love.
D. Sex attraction may mean that love also is present.
E. If there is no love there will be no sex attraction.

Sex relations are:

A. For physical pleasure.
B. A way to relieve tension.
C. A way to express love.
D. A biological urge.
E. All of the above.

Of the following, which one supplies the best evidence for predicting that a prospective husband or wife will be a good sex partner?

A. The "sex appeal" of the man or woman.
B. His or her interest in or conversation about sex.
C. His or her physical demonstrations of affection.
D. All of his or her behavior during courtship.
E. His or her response to physical closeness.

What is the probable reason[s] when muscles of a wife's vaginal entrance go into spasm, which may prevent intercourse altogether or cause her pain in intercourse?

A. Insufficient or inadequate sex play before intercourse.
B. No sex desire or inability to enjoy sex relations.
C. A learned involuntary reaction to sex relations as painful, dangerous.
D. Normal expectation that sex relations are threatening or painful.
E. An intentional act from fear of pregnancy or of intercourse.

How often is unsatisfactory intercourse caused by a difference in size of the male and female sex organs?

A. Almost always.
B. Very often.
C. Often.
D. At times.
E. Rarely.

What kind of intercourse is necessary for a woman to become pregnant?

A. She must reach orgasm before the man.
B. The man and woman must reach orgasm at the same time.
C. She must reach orgasm after the man.

D. Pregnancy is possible whenever sperm cells enter the vagina.
E. The man must reach orgasm for the pregnancy to be possible.

At what time in her cycle of menstruation is a woman most likely to become pregnant?

A. About two weeks before menstruation begins.
B. During the three days before menstruation begins.
C. During menstruation.
D. In the first day after menstruation begins.
E. During the first week after menstruation ends.*

The "Family History Analysis" is the newest tool to be used in premarital preparation. This eight page fill-in form is designed to help couples to become aware of how the families from which they have come will influence their own style of marriage. Each person brings to his or her own marriage a model of marriage—marital dreams, expectations, attitudes, and behaviors are not innate. Some will tend to repeat the pattern of their parents' marriage. Others will exercise energy and effort in trying to prevent their parents' marital dynamics from infiltrating their own. Thus they tend to behave and react in the opposite manner.

The "Family History Analysis" is given to the couple prior to the first session. It is returned to the minister or counselor so that he will have an opportunity to read through the form and make indications that are significant items. The forms are returned to the couple at the conclusion of the first session for them to discuss those items before they see the minister or counselor again. Often much of the content of the second session will involve information derived from the FHA. The value of this form is that it will help couples to become aware of their past and how it might affect their future. It will assist them in gaining the freedom to develop their own style of marriage. Listed here are some of the actual questions from this form so that you may see how it can be used.

Family History—Father and Mother

I would like to know about your father. (If you have a stepfather, please

*Used by permission.

describe the one you feel closest to or the one you regard as your father.)

1. List what you feel are the positive qualities of your father.
2. List what you feel are the negative qualities of your father.
3. Describe how you feel about your father.
4. What emotions does he express openly and how?
5. Describe how you and your father communicate.
6. Describe the most pleasant and unpleasant experiences with your father.
7. What was/is your father's goal for your life?

Describe on the following chart (by drawing a line graph) the history of your personal relationship with your mother from infancy to the present time.

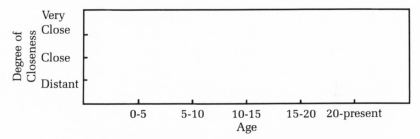

In making decisions or solving interpersonal conflicts, people use different styles of negotiation for handling conflict. Please indicate the style of each family member by placing a check mark in the appropriate column.

	WIN	LOSE	YIELD	WITHDRAW	RESOLVE
Yourself					
Father					
Mother					
Brother					
Brother					
Sister					
Sister					

Where on the following line would you place yourself currently in relationship to your parents?

COMPLETELY   COMPLETELY
DEPENDENT   INDEPENDENT

Who managed the finances in your family?

Describe how your mother and father demonstrated affection to one another and to you.

The FHA may be ordered from Family Counseling & Enrichment, 1913 E. 17th Street, Suite 118, Santa Ana, CA 92701.

The major test used in premarital counseling is the "Taylor-Johnson Temperament Analysis," (T-JTA).[1] In the January, 1973, issue of the *Family Coordinator*, Dr. Clinton Phillips published an article, "Some Useful Tests for Marriage Counselors." The Taylor-Johnson test was mentioned as one of the five tests. The American Institute of Family Relations in Hollywood has given this test to more than seventy thousand couples over the years, and thousands of other counselors and ministers have used it extensively. It is used for individual, premarital, marital, and family counseling, business and industry placement, placement of Sunday school teachers, evaluation of counselors for Christian camps, and assessment of college and seminary students. The test has been used as the basis for Bible studies in groups, as the traits lend themselves well to biblical teaching.

The test takes between thirty and forty-five minutes to complete. The profile derived from the test is very readable; lay people can understand it readily. Norms for the test are available for high school, college, and adult ages. It is important to remember that a minister must take a training course in order to qualify to administer and work with the test. Many seminaries give that training. Numerous one-day seminars are conducted throughout the United States, which qualify ministers and counselors to use this test. For information regarding a seminar in your area write to Christian Marriage Enrichment, 1913 E. 17th St., Suite 118, Santa Ana, CA 92701.

Before the couple comes for their first counseling session, they are asked to take the test. They may pick up the forms at the church office, or the forms may be mailed to them. The counselor goes over the instructions with them before they take the test. Each one takes it twice. The woman takes it as she sees herself. and then as she sees her fiancé. He takes the test as he sees himself and then as he sees her. That is called a criss-cross. The information derived from each person's perception of himself or herself and of the partner is invaluable and saves several hours of counseling.

Since many emotional problems such as uncontrolled anger, depression, worry, lack of empathy, or a low self-image are at the heart of numerous marital problems, it is crucial to take an intense look at that area for each person. Following are four profiles of a married couple, showing the scores for themselves and then the criss-cross. Look at the profiles, noting the nine traits and their definitions and the four shaded areas (from "excellent" to "improvement urgent"). Study the differences in which they both have strengths and weaknesses as well as problem areas between them.

By having the test returned to you before the couple's first session, you will have time to score the forms before you meet with them. Even though you do not go over the results until the individual sessions, you may want to probe into certain areas of their life or relationship because of what the tests have revealed.

One of the newest and most helpful tools is PREPARE II (PREmarital Personal and Relationship Evaluation), which is a scientifically developed instrument that is specifically designed to assess the personal and relationship strengths and problematic issues for couples.[2]

It has been designed as a diagnostic tool for professionals working with premarital couples in either educational or counseling programs.

PREPARE II is a 125-item procedure that assesses attitudes and personal issues in the following areas:

Communication
Conflict Resolution
Sexual Relationship
Financial Management
Realistic Expectations
Religious Orientation
Equalitarian Roles
Family and Friends
Children and Marriage
Personality Issues
Leisure Activities
Idealistic Distortion

HUSBAND

TAYLOR-JOHNSON TEMPERAMENT ANALYSIS PROFILE
Profile Revision of 1967

These Answers Describe **BROWN, RICHARD** _____ Age **46** Sex **M** Date **8-1-66**

School **U. OF CALIF.** Grade _____ Degree **PhD.** Major **CHEM. ENG.** Occupation **CHEM. ENGINEER** Counselor **W.E.**

Single ____ Years Married **20** Years Divorced ____ Years Widowed ____ Children: M **1** Ages **18** F **1** Ages **16**

Answers made by: SELF and/or husband, wife, father, mother, son, daughter, brother, sister, or _____ of the person described.

Norm(s): 67-68 GEN. POP.	A	B	C	D	E	F	G	H	I	Attitude (Sten) Score:
Mids		1	2	1		1			1	Total Mids: 6
Raw score	4	7	20	17	34	1	20	8	37	Raw score
Percentile	20	50	19	11	65	5	26	39	96	Percentile
TRAIT	Nervous	Depressive	Active-Social	Expressive-Responsive	Sympathetic	Subjective	Dominant	Hostile	Self-disciplined	TRAIT

| TRAIT OPPOSITE | Composed | Light-hearted | Quiet | Inhibited | Indifferent | Objective | Submissive | Tolerant | Impulsive | TRAIT OPPOSITE |

■ Excellent   ■ Acceptable   ▨ Improvement desirable   □ Improvement urgent

DEFINITIONS

TRAITS

Nervous — Tense, high-strung, apprehensive.
Depressive — Pessimistic, discouraged, dejected.
Active-Social — Energetic, enthusiastic, socially involved.
Expressive-Responsive — Spontaneous, affectionate, demonstrative.
Sympathetic — Kind, understanding, compassionate.
Subjective — Emotional, illogical, self-absorbed.
Dominant — Confident, assertive, competitive.
Hostile — Critical, argumentative, punitive.
Self-disciplined — Controlled, methodical, persevering.

OPPOSITES

Composed — Calm, relaxed, tranquil.
Light-hearted — Happy, cheerful, optimistic.
Quiet — Socially inactive, lethargic, withdrawn.
Inhibited — Restrained, unresponsive, repressed.
Indifferent — Unsympathetic, insensitive, unfeeling.
Objective — Fair-minded, reasonable, logical.
Submissive — Passive, compliant, dependent.
Tolerant — Accepting, patient, humane.
Impulsive — Uncontrolled, disorganized, changeable.

Note: Important decisions should not be made on the basis of this profile without confirmation of these results by other means.

Copyright ©1968 by Psychological Publications, Inc.
Reproduction in whole or part prohibited.   Published by Psychological Publications, Inc., 5300 Hollywood Blvd., Los Angeles, California 90027

1. *Taylor-Johnson Temperament Analysis* (T-JTA), Taylor, Robert M., and Morrison, Lucile Philips, by Psychological Publications, Inc., 5300 Hollywood Blvd., Los Angeles, CA 90027, 1966-74.

Printed by permission of Robert M. Taylor & Psychological Publications, Inc.

WIFE

TAYLOR-JOHNSON TEMPERAMENT ANALYSIS PROFILE
Profile Revision of 1967

These Answers Describe **BROWN, HELEN** _____ Age **40** ___ Sex **F** ___ Date **8-1-66**

School **COMPLETED** __ Grade **11** Degree _____ Major_____ Occupation **HOUSEWIFE** _____ Counselor **W.E.**

Single____ Years Married **20** Years Divorced____ Years Widowed____ Children: M **1** Ages **18** ____ F **1** Ages **16** _____

Answers made by: SELF $\frac{and}{or}$ husband, wife, father, mother, son, daughter, brother, sister, or_____of the person described.

Norm(s): 67-63 GEN. POP	A	B	C	D	E	F	G	H	I	Attitude (Sten) Score: 5
Mids		2		3	5	4			4	Total Mids: 19
Raw score	16	18	36	37	35	20	32	13	18	Raw score
Percentile	66	72	94	87	60	81	96	71	23	Percentile
TRAIT	Nervous	Depressive	Active-Social	Expressive-Responsive	Sympathetic	Subjective	Dominant	Hostile	Self-disciplined	TRAIT

TRAIT OPPOSITE	Composed	Light-hearted	Quiet	Inhibited	Indifferent	Objective	Submissive	Tolerant	Impulsive	TRAIT OPPOSITE

Excellent   Acceptable   Improvement desirable   Improvement urgent

DEFINITIONS

TRAITS

Nervous — Tense, high-strung, apprehensive.
Depressive — Pessimistic, discouraged, dejected.
Active-Social — Energetic, enthusiastic, socially involved.
Expressive-Responsive — Spontaneous, affectionate, demonstrative.
Sympathetic — Kind, understanding, compassionate.
Subjective — Emotional, illogical, self-absorbed.
Dominant — Confident, assertive, competitive.
Hostile — Critical, argumentative, punitive.
Self-disciplined — Controlled, methodical, persevering.

OPPOSITES

Composed — Calm, relaxed, tranquil.
Light-hearted — Happy, cheerful, optimistic.
Quiet — Socially inactive, lethargic, withdrawn.
Inhibited — Restrained, unresponsive, repressed.
Indifferent — Unsympathetic, insensitive, unfeeling.
Objective — Fair-minded, reasonable, logical.
Submissive — Passive, compliant, dependent.
Tolerant — Accepting, patient, humane.
Impulsive — Uncontrolled, disorganized, changeable.

Note: Important decisions should not be made on the basis of this profile without confirmation of these results by other means.

Copyright ⓒ1968 by Psychological Publications, Inc.
Reproduction in whole or part prohibited.   Published by Psychological Publications, Inc., 5300 Hollywood Blvd., Los Angeles, California 90027

Printed by permission of Robert M. Taylor & Psychological Publications, Inc.

HUSBAND ~~BY WIFE~~
CRISS - CROSS
TAYLOR-JOHNSON TEMPERAMENT ANALYSIS PROFILE
Profile Revision of 1967

These Answers Describe **BROWN, RICHARD**   Age **46**   Sex **M**   Date **8-1-66**

School **U OF CALIF.** Grade _____ Degree **Ph.D.** Major **CHEM. ENG.** Occupation **CHEM · ENGINEER**   Counselor **W.E.**

Single _____ Years Married **20** Years Divorced _____ Years Widowed _____ Children: M **1** Ages **18**   F **1** Ages **16**

Answers made by: SELF ⓐⓝⓓ husband, wife, father, mother, son, daughter, brother, sister, or _____ of the person described.

Norm(s) :67-68 G.P. c.c.	A		B		C		D		E		F		G		H		I		Attitude (Sten) Score: **6** **6**
Mids	**4**	**1**	**2**		**2**	**2**	**1**			**1**	**1**	**1**		**2**			**1**	**1**	Total Mids: **6** **13**
Raw score	**4**	**10**	**7**	**8**	**20**	**12**	**17**	**6**	**34**	**19**	**1**	**9**	**20**	**10**	**8**	**2**	**37**	**37**	Raw score
Percentile	**20**	**36**	**50**	**39**	**19**	**13**	**11**	**2**	**65**	**23**	**5**	**36**	**26**	**9**	**39**	**9**	**96**	**95**	Percentile
TRAIT	Nervous		Depressive		Active-Social		Expressive-Responsive		Sympathetic		Subjective		Dominant		Hostile		Self-disciplined		TRAIT

95										95
90										90
85										85
80										80
75										75
70										70
65										65
60										60
55										55
50										50
45										45
40										40
35										35
30										30
25										25
20										20
15										15
10										10
5										5

| TRAIT OPPOSITE | Composed | Light-hearted | Quiet | Inhibited | Indifferent | Objective | Submissive | Tolerant | Impulsive | TRAIT OPPOSITE |

Excellent	Acceptable	Improvement desirable	Improvement urgent

DEFINITIONS

TRAITS

Nervous — Tense, high-strung, apprehensive.
Depressive — Pessimistic, discouraged, dejected.
Active-Social — Energetic, enthusiastic, socially involved.
Expressive-Responsive — Spontaneous, affectionate, demonstrative.
Sympathetic — Kind, understanding, compassionate.
Subjective — Emotional, illogical, self-absorbed.
Dominant — Confident, assertive, competitive.
Hostile — Critical, argumentative, punitive.
Self-disciplined — Controlled, methodical, persevering.

OPPOSITES

Composed — Calm, relaxed, tranquil.
Light-hearted — Happy, cheerful, optimistic.
Quiet — Socially inactive, lethargic, withdrawn.
Inhibited — Restrained, unresponsive, repressed.
Indifferent — Unsympathetic, insensitive, unfeeling.
Objective — Fair-minded, reasonable, logical.
Submissive — Passive, compliant, dependent.
Tolerant — Accepting, patient, humane.
Impulsive — Uncontrolled, disorganized, changeable.

Note: Important decisions should not be made on the basis of this profile without confirmation of these results by other means.

Copyright ©1968 by Psychological Publications, Inc.
Reproduction in whole or part prohibited.   Published by Psychological Publications, Inc., 5300 Hollywood Blvd., Los Angeles, California 90027

Printed by permission of Robert M. Taylor & Psychological Publications, Inc.

WIFE BY HUSBAND

CRISS - CROSS

TAYLOR-JOHNSON TEMPERAMENT ANALYSIS PROFILE
Profile Revision of 1967

These Answers Describe **BROWN, HELEN**   Age **40**   Sex **F**   Date **8-1-66**

School **COMPLETED**   Grade **11**   Degree_____ Major_____   Occupation **HOUSEWIFE**   Counselor **W.E.**

Single_____ Years Married **20** Years Divorced_____ Years Widowed_____ Children: M **1** Ages **18**   F **1** Ages **16**

Answers made by: SELF **and** husband, wife, father, mother, son, daughter, brother, sister, or_____of the person described.

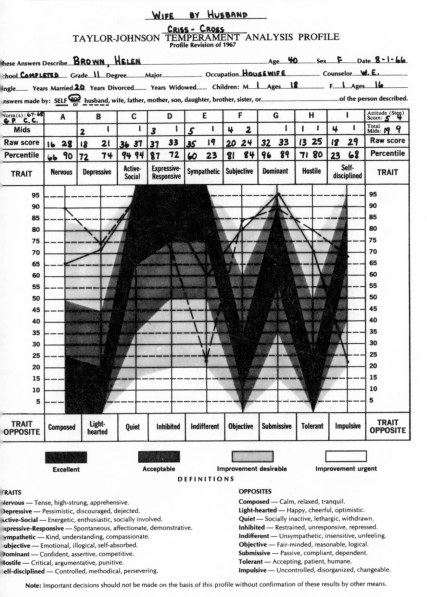

Norm(s): 67-68 G.P. C.C.	A		B		C		D		E		F		G		H		I		Attitude (Step) Score: **5** **4**
Mids		2	1		1	3	1		5	1	4	2		1	1	1	4	1	Total Mids: **19** **9**
Raw score	16	28	18	21	36	37	37	33	35	19	20	24	32	33	13	25	18	29	Raw score
Percentile	66	90	72	74	94	94	87	72	60	23	81	84	96	89	71	80	23	68	Percentile
TRAIT	Nervous		Depressive		Active-Social		Expressive-Responsive		Sympathetic		Subjective		Dominant		Hostile		Self-disciplined		TRAIT

TRAIT OPPOSITE	Composed	Light-hearted	Quiet	Inhibited	Indifferent	Objective	Submissive	Tolerant	Impulsive	TRAIT OPPOSITE

Excellent   Acceptable   Improvement desirable   Improvement urgent

DEFINITIONS

TRAITS

Nervous — Tense, high-strung, apprehensive.
Depressive — Pessimistic, discouraged, dejected.
Active-Social — Energetic, enthusiastic, socially involved.
Expressive-Responsive — Spontaneous, affectionate, demonstrative.
Sympathetic — Kind, understanding, compassionate.
Subjective — Emotional, illogical, self-absorbed.
Dominant — Confident, assertive, competitive.
Hostile — Critical, argumentative, punitive.
Self-disciplined — Controlled, methodical, persevering.

OPPOSITES

Composed — Calm, relaxed, tranquil.
Light-hearted — Happy, cheerful, optimistic.
Quiet — Socially inactive, lethargic, withdrawn.
Inhibited — Restrained, unresponsive, repressed.
Indifferent — Unsympathetic, insensitive, unfeeling.
Objective — Fair-minded, reasonable, logical.
Submissive — Passive, compliant, dependent.
Tolerant — Accepting, patient, humane.
Impulsive — Uncontrolled, disorganized, changeable.

Note: Important decisions should not be made on the basis of this profile without confirmation of these results by other means.

Copyright ©1968 by Psychological Publications, Inc.
Reproduction in whole or part prohibited.   Published by Psychological Publications, Inc., 5300 Hollywood Blvd., Los Angeles, California 90027

Printed by permission of Robert M. Taylor & Psychological Publications, Inc.

It is computerized so that results can be readily obtained and accurately scored. A 7-10 page computer analysis is provided, which is easily interpreted. Results are returned within one week from the time they are received.

PREPARE II results provide individual (male and female) scores and couple scores for each of the twelve categories. Individual percentile scores and revised percentile scores that correct for an individual "faking good" are provided. Couple agreement and disagreement scores are provided to indicate potential strengths and problematic areas for couples. Both individual and couple scores are compared with continually updated norms based on all couples who have taken PREPARE II.

Also listed are all the disagreement, special focus, and indecision items. The entire sentence and couple scores are fully printed for each of these items. A counselor's manual describes how to interpret and use the computerized results with couples.

The following is a description of the areas covered within that analysis.

- *Idealistic Distortion*

This category is a modified version of Edmonds (1967) Marital Conventionalization Scale. This scale has been well validated and correlates highly with other scales that measure the tendency of individuals to answer personal questions in a socially desirable direction. Since premarital couples tend to be highly idealistic, this scale is intended to assess the degree to which individuals attempt to present themselves in a highly favorable and often exaggerated way. Moderately high scores identify individuals who are responding in a way that presents a favorable impression of their relationship. Questions are extreme and therefore reflect a tendency that in all likelihood permeates the entire inventory and must be carefully attended.

- *Realistic Expectations*

This category assesses the rational quality of an individual's expectations about marriage, love, commitment, and relationship conflicts. The intent of these items is to ascertain the degree to which expectations about marriage relationships are realistic and grounded in objective reflection. Low scores would suggest that individuals are too romantic or idealistic in their perception of marriage. In general, moderately high scores in this category reflect realistic expectations about relationship issues.

- *Personality Issues*

This category assesses an individual's perception of the personality characteristics of his partner and the level of satisfaction or dissatisfaction with that perception. Items focus on traits such as sense of humor, temper, moodiness, stubbornness, jealousy, and possessiveness. Personal behaviors related to demonstration of affection, smoking, and drinking are also included. Moderately high scores in this category are intended to reflect personal adjustment to partner and approval of partner's behavior.

- *Equalitarian Roles*

This category assesses an individual's beliefs and feelings about various marital and family roles. Items include occupational roles, household roles, sex roles, and parental roles. Individuals respond to these questions and reveal information about their satisfaction with assuming particular role behaviors. There is an implied bias in the scale toward equalitarian versus traditional role behaviors. For that reason, moderately high scores would reflect flexibility and satisfaction with equalitarian role positions. Moderately low scores would reflect a more traditional role position and may or may not be problematic for the couples.

- *Communication*

This category is concerned with an individual's feelings, beliefs, and attitudes toward the role of communication in the maintenance of marital relationships. Items focus on the ability of respondents to express important emotions and beliefs, the ability to listen to one's partner, the ability to respond appropriately in certain situations, and on the style or pattern of communication that exists between partners. Moderately high scores reflect an awareness of the communication skills necessary to maintain a relationship and an ability to use them.

- *Conflict Resolution*

This category assesses an individual's attitudes, feelings, and beliefs toward the existence and resolution of conflict in relationships. Items pertain to strategies used to end arguments, satisfaction with the way problems are resolved, and the openness of relationship partners to recognize and resolve issues. Moderately high scores reflect realistic attitudes about the probability of relationship conflicts and satisfaction with the way most problems are handled.

- *Financial Management*

This category focuses on attitudes and concerns about the way economics are to be managed in the family. Items assess the tendencies of individuals to be spenders or savers, the care in which financial decisions on major purchases are made, and decisions regarding the person or persons who will be in charge of specific financial matters. Satisfaction with economic status and responsibility for money management is indirectly assessed. Moderately high scores reflect satisfaction with financial management and realistic attitudes toward financial matters.

- *Leisure Activities*

This category assesses each individual's preferences for spending free time. Items reflect social versus personal activities, active versus passive interests, shared versus individual preferences, and expectations as to whether leisure time should be spent together or balanced between separate and joint activities. Moderately high scores reflect compatibility, flexibility, and/or consensus about the use of leisure time activities.

- *Sexual Relationship*

This category assesses individual feelings and concerns about the affectional and sexual relationship with the partner. Items reflect satisfaction with expressions of affection, level of comfort in discussion of sexual issues, attitudes toward sexual behavior and intercourse, birth control decisions, and feelings about sexual fidelity. Moderately high scores reflect satisfaction with affectional expressions and a positive attitude about the role of sexuality in marriage.

Here is a sampling of some of the 125 questions.

RESPONSE CHOICES

1. **Strongly Agree**
2. **Moderately Agree**
3. **Neither Agree nor Disagree**
4. **Moderately Disagree**
5. **Strongly Disagree**

1. I sometimes feel pressured to participate in activities that my partner enjoys.
2. It is very easy for me to express all my true feelings to my partner.
3. It is hard for me to have complete faith in some of the accepted practices of our religion.
4. In order to end an argument, I usually give in.
5. I am satisfied with how we have defined the responsibilities of a father in raising children.
6. When we are having a problem, my partner often gives me the silent treatment.
7. Some relatives or friends have reservations about our marriage.
8. There are times when I am bothered by my partner's jealousy.
9. I am completely satisfied with the amount of affection my partner gives me.
10. I would not seek help from a professional even if we had serious marital problems.
11. Religion should have the same meaning for both of us.

The computer printout clearly shows areas of disagreement as well as the couple's overall scores.

Here is a sample printout of the overall scores and their comparison with the norms.

SUMMARY ANALYSIS FOR PREPARE CATEGORIES

| | Individual Scores | | | | Couple Scores | | | | |
| | Male | | Female | | Item Summary | | | Positive Agreement | |
Category Title	Pct	Revised	Pct	Revised	Agree Items	Disagree Items	Indecision Items	Couple	Norm
Idealistic Distortion	78.		20.	***					
Realistic Expectations	22.	18.	84.	80.	1	6	3	10.	34.
Personality Issues	88.	70.	10.	10.	4	5	1	20.	35.
Equalitarian Roles	10.	10.	10.	10.	8	1	1	20.	44.
Communication	72.	60.	19.	17.	5	4	1	50.	47.
Conflict Resolution	82.	75.	15.	14.	3	2	5	30.	45.
Financial Management	26.	23.	35.	34.	4	4	2	40.	34.
Leisure Activities	94.	91.	75.	74.	7	1	2	70.	52.
Sexual Relationship	45.	42.	45.	44.	4	2	4	40.	47.
Children and Marriage	91.	81.	88.	85.	7	2	1	60.	39.
Family and Friends	66.	58.	59.	57.	7	0	3	60.	47.
Religious Orientation	12.	10.	10.	10.	8	1	1	30.	34.
Average Positive Agreement								39.	42.

Percentile Scores—Pct—range from 0 to 100 and have an average score of 50. Moderately high scores (60 or more) reflect positive relationship attitudes and adjustment. Revised scores are an adjustment of an individual's pct score based on each person's tendency to present an idealistic image of their relationship. Revised scores will be low when individuals are unrealistic about marriage. Positive agreement scores reflect partners consensus on attitudes believed to be related to positive adjustment in marriage. Relationship strengths are identified when a couple's positive agreement score is higher than the norm score for that category.

SPECIAL SITUATIONS

Category Title	Individual Scores					Couple Scores				
	Male		Female			Item Summary			Positive Agreement	
	Pct	Revised	Pct	Revised		Agree Items	Disagree Items	Indecision Items	Couple	Norm
Personality Issues	83	79	24	19	* * * *	5	3	2	20.	35.
Equalitarian Roles	27	24	17	14		9	0	1	10.	44.
Religious Orientation	19	16	17	13		8	1	1	20.	34.

The Male—high score—has positive perception of partner and general approval of partner's behavior.
The Female—low score—perceives her partner as having negative personality traits.
The low Positive Agreement also indicates that this may be a problematic area.
    *See p. 6 for listing of Items for Discussion for Personality Issues

The low Individual Scores and low Positive Agreement indicate that this couple do not desire an equal role in their family relationship and would prefer a more traditional approach. Their high Agreement would suggest that this may not create a problem for them.
    *See p. 12 of the Counselor's Manual for an explanation of the implied bias in this scale toward equalitarian versus traditional role behaviors.

The low Individual scores may mean that both partners regard religion as a personal decision or question traditional beliefs. This may not be a problematic area, however, as indicated by their high total of Agree Items.
    *See p. 14 of the Counselor's Manual for an explanation of the implied bias in this category toward traditional view of religion as an important component of marriage versus an individualistic interpretation.

STUDY THE CATEGORY DESCRIPTIONS

ALWAYS WATCH FOR THEMES AND PATTERNS

PERSONALITY ISSUES

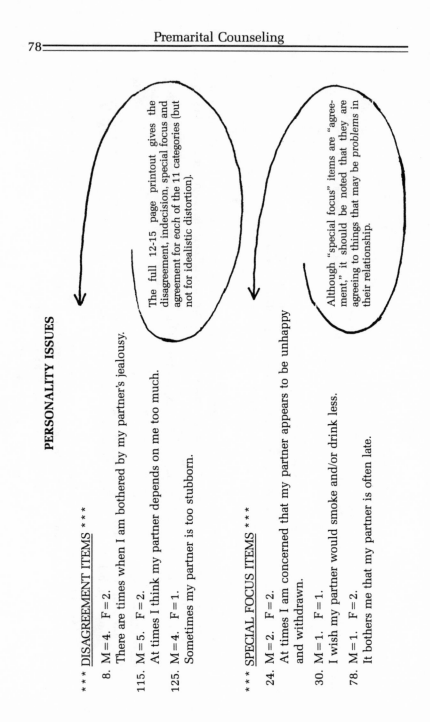

The full 12-15 page printout gives the disagreement, indecision, special focus and agreement for each of the 11 categories (but not for idealistic distortion).

Although "special focus" items are "agreement," it should be noted that they are agreeing to things that may be *problems in their relationship.*

*** DISAGREEMENT ITEMS ***

8. M = 4.   F = 2.
   There are times when I am bothered by my partner's jealousy.

115. M = 5.   F = 2.
   At times I think my partner depends on me too much.

125. M = 4.   F = 1.
   Sometimes my partner is too stubborn.

*** SPECIAL FOCUS ITEMS ***

24. M = 2.   F = 2.
   At times I am concerned that my partner appears to be unhappy and withdrawn.

30. M = 1.   F = 1.
   I wish my partner would smoke and/or drink less.

78. M = 1.   F = 2.
   It bothers me that my partner is often late.

*** COUPLE INDECISION ITEMS ***

37. M = 3. F = 3.
At times I am uncomfortable with the way my partner touches me in public.

95. M = 4. F = 3.
Sometimes I have difficulty dealing with my partner's moodiness.

POSITIVE
*** COUPLE AGREEMENT ITEMS ***

13. M = 4. F = 4. 44. M = 4. F = 5.

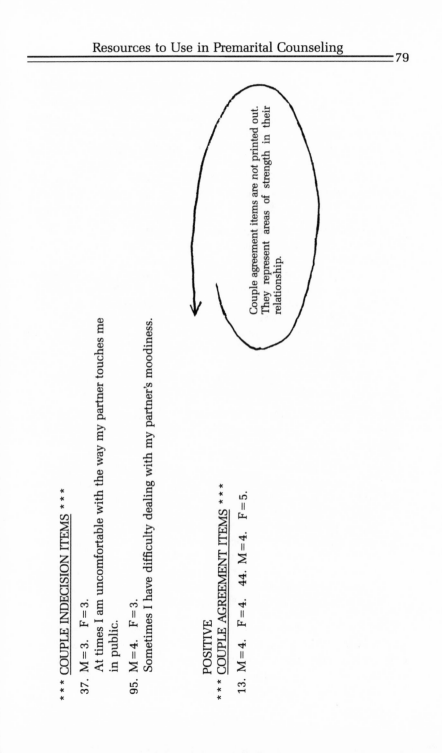

Couple agreement items are not printed out. They represent areas of strength in their relationship.

It is necessary to complete a training course in order to use this tool. (Contact Christian Marriage Enrichment for information. See p. 66). This resource is extremely helpful in identifying potential conflict areas that may be missed during the sessions. PREPARE II can also be used for marriage enrichment seminars and sessions.

Family Life Publications (Box 427, Saluda, SC 28773) has produced another form titled the *Marriage Expectation Inventory for Engaged Couples*. A sampling of the questions is listed here.

1. Loving my future partner means for me . . .
2. Recall four instances of how your future partner demonstrated love toward you during the last month:
3. List four situations in which you, intentionally or unintentionally, were hurtful to your future partner in the last month:
4. List two ways you and your future spouse differ:
5. List two ways you and your future spouse are alike:
6. List four things your future partner has "bugged" you about recently which you could have corrected, but did not.
7. Explain why.
8. What is the best strength you will bring to your marriage?
9. What is your future partner's best strength?

The "Premarital Counseling Inventory" has been developed by Research Press. The instructions on this form give the best explanation of its use:

This inventory asks several series of questions aimed at describing who you are, what you like about your present relationship, and how you would like to see it evolve. Based upon your thoughtful answers to these questions, the counselor can help you to determine your level of satisfaction with things as they are now. You can also be helped to redefine, together, some aspects of your relationship which could be improved. Based upon this information, you may be able to make a more confident decision about whether to marry or you may be able to strengthen the decision which you have already made.

Topic areas covered in this inventory are family background, past marital history, history of your present relationship, attitudes concerning roles, time, and money, and development of marital contract. Here is a sample section from this inventory, titled "History of Your Present Relationship."

III. History of your present relationship
    A. When did you first meet?
    B. For how many years and months have you known each other?
    C. What five strong points attract you to the other person?
    D. Have you decided to marry? Yes_____No_____. If no, please go on to question E. If yes, please answer the following questions.
        1. How confident are you about the wisdom of your decision?
           Very much so_____ Pretty confident_____
           Have some doubt_____ Very unsure_____
        2. What reaction have your parents had to your decision?
           Very positive_____ Positive_____ Neutral_____
           Negative_____
        3. What reaction have your friends had to your decision?
           Very positive_____ Positive_____ Neutral_____
           Negative_____
    E. Have you ever called off your plans to marry?
       Yes_____ No_____. If no, please go on to question F.
       If yes, please answer the following questions.
       1. When did this happen?
       2. What would you say was the cause?
       3. How did you resolve the situation?

. . . .

    G. Please list three ways in which you think a positive and specific change in the behavior of the other person would help you to enjoy your relationship more. For example, please write "Ask me how I spent my day" (positive and specific), rather than "Don't ignore me" (negative and vague).

	Is this:			
	Very important		Unimportant	
1. _____	1	2	3	4
1. _____	1	2	3	4
1. _____	1	2	3	4

    H. What are your three most important personal interests?
    I. What are the three things which you and your friend most enjoy doing together?

A final resource that is helpful in the area of communication is the "Premarital Communication Inventory" developed by Dr. Millard J. Bienvenu, Sr. This form must be ordered directly from the author at Northwestern State University of Louisiana, Natchitoches, LA 71457. A few of the questions will give you an idea of the contents of this discussion tool designed for the couple to use by themselves or with the pastor.

	Yes Usually	Sel- dom	Some- times
Do you have a tendency to keep your feelings to yourself?			
Does your fiancé tell you when he/she is angry with you?			
Does your fiancé fail to ask your opinion in making plans involving the two of you?			
Do you communicate successfully with each other's families?			
Does it bother you unduly for your fiancé to express his/ her own beliefs if they differ from yours?			
Does your fiancé nag you?			
Does your fiancé wait until you are through talking before saying what he/she has to say?			
Do the two of you discuss what you expect of one another in terms of a future mother and father?			

One final area must be noted: the cost of counseling. Is there any charge when it is done at the church? What would it cost if the couple went to a professional marriage counselor? In answer to the second question, it would cost a couple between $90.00 and $200.00 for that preparation. Most churches do not charge for counseling. However, the wedding service fee usually pays for church use, utilities, janitorial service, and other expenses. A number of churches have begun to include an additional twenty-five or thirty-dollar fee to cover the cost of counseling. That money pays for the books that the pastor gives to the couple. It is important for the couple to own the books. Many have stated that after they were married they reread the books, which took on a new meaning for them. The fee also pays for the testing materials used by the couple and several series of tapes used in the counseling ministry.

One final word of instruction is necessary. Before proceeding with the ministry of counseling, the pastor or lay person must be totally familiar with the tapes, books, tests, and other materials to be used. It may take several weeks of study, but that in turn enhances the ministry of marital preparation. In addition to reading the books already mentioned, a pastor or counselor will benefit greatly and add depth to his counseling ministry by reading the following books. Remember that those authors hold various views, and the reader will not agree with everything they say. That will be beneficial since it will cause the reader to think and to examine his beliefs.

NOTES

1. *Taylor-Johnson Temperament Analysis* (T-JTA), Taylor, Robert M., and Morrison, Lucile Philips, by Psychological Publications, Inc., 5300 Hollywood Blvd., Los Angeles, CA 90027, 1966-74.
2. Used by permission of PREPARE Inc. Additional information may be obtained by writing to PREPARE Inc., P.O. Box 190, Minneapolis, MN 55440.

BIBLIOGRAPHY

Hollis, Harry Jr. *Thank God for Sex*. Nashville: Broadman, 1975.

Jackson, Don, and Lederer, William. *The Mirages of Marriage*. New York: Norton, 1968.

Roman, Mel, and Raley, Patricia. *The Indelible Family*. New York: Rawson Wade, 1980.

Small, Dwight H. *Marriage as Equal Partnership*. Grand Rapids: Baker, 1980.

Swindoll, Charles. *Strike the Original Match*. Portland, Ore.: Multnomah Press, 1980.

Yancy, Philip. *After the Wedding*. Waco, Tex.: Word, 1976.

5

The First and Second Sessions

The first session is about to begin. The couple is arriving at the church for their first premarital interview. Prior to this session they have completed the "Taylor-Johnson Temperament Analysis" and "PREPARE II." They have also answered individually several questions that will be covered in that particular session. The questions were given or mailed to them along with the PREPARE and Taylor-Johnson test. The following questions should be answered before the session (these questions should not be discussed between the couple prior to the session):

1. What is your definition of marriage?
2. How were feelings of love, warmth, and tenderness shown in your home as you were growing up? How would you like feelings of love, warmth, and tenderness shown to you in public and in your home?
3. What fears and concerns do you have about marriage?
4. List in writing ten specific indications as to why this is the time of your life to marry. List in writing twelve specific reasons why you want to marry the other person. (I also give instructions for taking the Taylor-Johnson Temperament Analysis and PRE-PARE tests.)

Other questions are posed during the counseling session.

After the couple arrives, it is important to spend time getting acquainted. Some of the couples will be people a pastor has known for years, others will be strangers. It is helpful for the pastor to share information about himself such as background, family, hobbies, schools, and some of his interesting experiences in marriage.

One of the basic ground rules of the premarital counseling is stated in the beginning: there is nothing that cannot be discussed in those sessions. The couple should not hesitate to ask the pastor any questions they have, and he will take the same privilege of asking them anything he thinks necessary.

It is important to remind the couple of the agreement that they complete their outside assignments if the counseling is to continue. I ask them to share their expectations for premarital counseling with me.

The session is then under way with the question, "Why are you coming to the church to be married, instead of going to a justice of the peace?" Why is a church important? Such a question helps the couple clarify their motivation for being married in the church and causes them to think of the testimonial aspect of the wedding ceremony. Perhaps they have to verbalize their reasons for the first time. This may be a new revelation to each of them. For some individuals the church has little or no meaning. Others are very committed to having Jesus Christ at the center of their marriage relationship.

Next they are asked to share their definition of marriage. That they do individually. At this point the pastor can share several definitions of marriage with them, his own and others that have been formulated. There are many definitions that could be explained at this point; sometimes they are incorporated into the wedding itself. One was written by David Augsburger:

> Is marriage a private action of two persons in love, or a public act of two pledging a contract? Neither, it is something other. Very much other! Basically, the Christian view of marriage is not that it is primarily or essentially a binding legal and social contract. The Christian understands marriage as a covenant made under God and in the presence of fellow members of the Christian Family. Such a pledge endures, not because of the force of law or the fear of its sanctions, but because an unconditional covenant has been

made. A convenant more solemn, more binding, more permanent than any legal contract.[1]

Another interesting definition was shared in a message by Dr. David Hubbard:

> Marriage does not demand perfection. But it must be given priority. It is an institution for sinners. No one else need apply. But it finds its finest glory when sinners see it as God's way of leading us through His ultimate curriculum of love and righteousness.[2]

The definition that I have been formulating for several years is the one that I concentrate on with the couple. It is given here, followed by an amplification that I share in counseling and in classes with married couples. This will give you an example of the personal aspect of this counseling.

> A Christian marriage is a total commitment of two people to the person of Jesus Christ and to one another. It is a commitment in which there is no holding back of anything. Marriage is a pledge of mutual fidelity; it is a partnership of mutual subordination. A Christian marriage is similar to a solvent, a freeing up of the man and woman to be themselves and become all that God intends for them to become. Marriage is the refining process that God will use to have us develop into the man or woman He wants us to become.
>
> There is one phrase there that I would like to focus on; this phrase is "the refining process." Have you ever thought of your marriage as a refining process? That God is going to allow certain events to happen in your life that will cause you to grow and develop into the man or woman He wants you to become? What would happen if you were to have that attitude toward the events that occur within your marriage—that those events are something that God can use to cause you to grow deeper together and to cause each to grow more as an individual?
>
> Each of you has had different experiences. In every marriage it will be different. We've had a unique situation in our relationship. We have two children, a daughter who is twenty, and a son who is fourteen years of age. He's about eighteen months old mentally and will probably never be more than three or four years old mentally. He is a brain-damaged, mentally retarded child. When Matthew was first born we didn't know this. At about eight months of age, he began having seizures. We took him to the UCLA medical clinic where the diagnosis was made.

The name "Matthew" means "God's gift," or "gift from God." Matthew is God's gift to us. We have experienced times of pain, disappointment, and heartache, but we've experienced other times of joy and delight. I can remember when we prayed for Matthew to walk. All of us in our family prayed for about three and a half years. And one day when we were together, he stood up and took about five steps. I said something like, "Isn't that wonderful?" Joyce said something like, "Isn't that great?" Then our nine-year-old daughter said, "Let's stop right now and thank God for answering our prayer." It is interesting how our children will teach us and will cause us to give thanks to the proper person.

You consider some of the events that may occur in your life and you wonder, "How in the world am I going to handle them when I don't even know what's going to happen?" But God gives us the resources to handle whatever happens; He does this in His wonderful and marvelous way, even when we're not aware of it. God can be preparing us for some of those situations that are going to hit us.

Before Matthew was born and I was in seminary, I had to write a thesis. I didn't know what to write about. When I went in, the professor said to me, "Nobody's written a thesis on the Christian education of the mentally retarded child. You write it." So I did. I read books, studied, went to schools, and observed Sunday school classes for these children. I learned a lot about them. Then I wrote the thesis.

My wife typed the thesis the first time, a second time, and finally a third time, and she learned about retarded children as well. After it was finally turned in and accepted, I went to work at my church while I was working on a psychology degree. I had to do an internship in the public school district for the school psychologist credential. I was assigned to test and re-test mentally retarded children. At my church I was given the responsibility of training teachers to teach mentally retarded children within the church, and so I had to develop a program.

One night two years before Matthew was born, Joyce and I were talking; we said, "Isn't it interesting all the experience we've had with retarded children? Could it be that God is preparing us for something that is going to occur later in our life?" That is all we said. Two years later Matthew came into our lives. We saw how God prepared us.

When an event occurs in your life that some would call a tragedy, can you look back and see how God has been preparing you for that, or how He's going to give you the extra strength, wisdom, and patience right at the right time for you to handle it? Marriage is a refining process. An adequate concept of what marriage is about is the first foundation of marriage preparation.

There are occasions when I ask the couple for their definitions but do not share others with them at that point. They will be hearing the definition of marriage and the experience of Matthew in the tape series "Enriching Your Marriage."

The next topic area which we explore is the couple's individual family background. For example, the woman (and then the man) could be asked to share something about her home and family, such as where she lived, in what type of home, what her parents did, whether they are still together, whether she has brothers and sisters and what type of relationships they have, the financial status of the home, whether the family moved around or lived in one place. She also answers the following question: How did your parents' physical and mental health relate to you in growing up? How did your parents handle disagreements? Which parent did you admire the most?

A very important question to ask is, Is there any way in which there is a dependency and/or something unresolved between you and your parents?

It is important to learn the number of brothers and sisters and their own position in the family order. Were they the oldest, youngest, or middle child? Were they the oldest of brothers or sisters? If they were the youngest, were the others brothers or sisters? For example, if the man is the oldest child and had three younger sisters, and the woman was the oldest child and had younger brothers, how might that affect the marital relationship? Suppose the woman were the oldest sister of brothers and the man was the youngest child in his family and had older sisters. How will that affect the marriage? Similar questions are posed to the couple to let them consider the possible influence of family position. There is a theory that states that sibling positions can be looked upon as roles that a person has learned to take in the family and has the tendency to assume in situations outside of the family. They may be quite similar or modified. That theory is discussed in detail in *Family Constellation* by Walter Toman (New York: Springer, 1976, 3rd ed.). That is theory and not an absolute fact; yet it does warrant consideration, especially in establishing a marital relationship. In the book, specific characteristics of each person's position are given such as: what an older brother of brothers is like, what a middle child is like, what a younger sister of sisters is like, and so on. For purpose of illustration, here is a sampling of the suggestions of some of the best and worst matches for a marital relationship ("the worst" meaning having the greatest potential for conflict and adjustment problems.)

An oldest brother of brothers would be best matched with a younger sister of sisters. The worst match would be with an older sister of sisters.

A youngest brother of brothers would be best matched with an older sister of brothers, but the worst match would be marrying an only child.

An only male would be best matched with either an older sister of sisters or an older sister of brothers, but the worst would be marrying a female only child.

Before working with or applying this theory it is important to study thoroughly the afore-mentioned book.

Two questions are asked that the couple were requested to answer in writing before the session: How were feelings of love, warmth, and tenderness shown in your home as you were growing up? How would you like feelings of love, warmth, and tenderness shown to you in public and in your home?

Part of the problem you are looking for is the fact that when people come out of their own homes they might carry with them some of the behavior that was detrimental in that home. They also might have certain expectations. For example, a person might come into marriage with the expectation that his or her mate will be like a parent whom he or she admired. Or, one partner may have the expectation that the mate will not be like a parent with whom this individual had a number of differences. One may believe that the life-style in the new home will be the same as in the parental home; another may wish it to be radically different.

There is also the problem that a person might have a personal conviction that his or her description of a mate and a parent is the only acceptable description. He or she will not allow latitude for the other person's ideas and perceptions; this inflexibility can create difficulties later in the marriage relationship. An example may illustrate this.

The young man's name was Bob. His mother died in childbirth. He had no brothers or sisters. He was reared solely by his father and had no contact with women in his home as he was growing up. His father was lower middle class. They moved every year or two. Bob went to many different schools, lived in different cities all over the nation, and had no settled roots.

Bob did not date very much. When he was in high school he dated a girl only once or twice. Later he went to college by himself. He worked very hard; he spent a lot of time studying, and a lot of time working at a job. When he was twenty-three years of age, he met a young woman named Janet; they fell in love and decided to be married.

Janet came from an upper middle-class home. The family had lived in the same location for the past fifteen years. Janet had two brothers and three sisters. The family was very stable. They did many things together; they were a very close-knit group. The grandparents lived nearby, and there were aunts and uncles in the same town. Janet never had to want for much. She had money when she needed it, and the parents took a great deal of interest in all their children.

Here was a couple with great differences in their backgrounds. Premarital counseling was vital for them. There were some major differences that needed to be explored, for the marriage could have suffered greatly because of those differences. The young man had had very little contact with females. He did not know what it is like to live in a home with women around. He did not have a mother or any sisters, and he did not date much, so after marriage he could have been in for a very real cultural shock. He had not had much experience in sharing a home with other individuals. What happens when he is married? In the morning he walks into the bathroom and runs into nylons drying on the towel rack. He realizes that he is living with a person who is very different than himself.

If he is very frugal and she is accustomed to spending money freely, what conflicts will come about? An unfortunate factor in this situation is that, at least from what we know, this young man did not have a good model of what a family should be like.

Those are just a *few* of the areas of adjustment. The couple must be made aware of differences and must be asked to develop a plan and approach to solve these potential problems.

Another topic is the dating background of this couple: How long have they been going together, and what kind of dates have they had? For example, here are two different couples. One couple has been dating for the past two and one-half years. They live in the same town. Their dates occur mostly on Friday and Saturday nights, and sometimes on Sunday evenings. During the week they have very little contact with one another. Quite often when they go out on Friday or Saturday night they go to a movie or some type of entertainment. Now and then they go to a party, but they really do not have that much time to communicate with one another.

On the other hand, a couple may have a completely different history. They have been dating and thinking seriously about marriage. They have been dating for eight months, but during that period they have spent quite a few hours together each day. During the summer they worked together washing dishes in the kitchen of a Christian camp, and they saw each other at times when they were happy, when they felt sad, and when they were in bad moods. All of that contributed to a good relationship.

Now as you look at the two couples, you might think, "Well, there's a couple who has gone together for over two years. They might have a better relationship." That is not necessarily true. The couple who spent more varied and realistic time together, even though the time was shorter, could have a better adjustment.

The couple to be counseled should be asked what they have done on their dates, where they have gone, whether they have included other friends, or if they have just gone places alone. It is also important that each individual has become acquainted with the other's parents. In fact, young couples who are seriously dating should be encouraged to spend time in the evenings in each other's parents' homes. On some occasions I have met couples whose families have gotten together on vacations and all spent a week together in the mountains. This has contributed to a healthy relationship.

Recently a couple who came for premarital counseling had a unique experience to share along that line. He was twenty-nine and she was twenty-six. He was a lawyer in Los Angeles, and she held a job with a Christian organization in Seattle, Washington.

Several months before the wedding he drove to Seattle to spend time with her, and they decided to take a week together and tour Vancouver, British Columbia. That would mean that they would spend several days together in close contact under varied conditions. Prior to their trip, they discussed it in depth and planned where they would go and what they would do. They also determined that on that trip they would not so much as hold hands, as they did not want to allow for any possibility of difficulty occurring in their physical relationship. At night they obtained separate motel rooms.

They made that commitment, prayed together, and enjoyed their trip. This couple had a deep commitment to the Lord and to one another. It was a delight to work with a couple such as that in counseling. Not every couple could or should have that type of experience. But realistic dating is essential.

An additional question to ask at this point is, "In what way will the type of courtship you have had contribute to your marriage?"

The fifth area that is discussed can be delicate. We should be concerned about the extent of their sexual involvement and the attitude the couple has toward this important aspect of their relationship. This topic may be introduced by asking each of them about the sexual information that has been given to them over the years: Who prepared you in terms of your understanding about sex? Who talked with you? What books have you read?

One of the questions I ask, that quite often brings on a silence, is this: "Most couples desire to express their affection in some physical manner. To what extent have you had the opportunity to express your affection to one another?"

I have experienced various responses to asking the initial question ranging from, "Why do you want to know?", to long silences, guilty looks, and positive statement of "We kiss and hold each other a lot and really enjoy our time together." One couple confided that they allowed themselves ten minutes of kissing, holding, and hugging and then stopped, since during that time span they could control themselves. They said after that they seemed to run into difficulty. If I do not get any response from the couple at that particular time, then I might go a little more into detail by explaining that when a couple is in love they have certain feelings toward each other and they like to express those feelings sexually. Now I may get continued silence from a couple. Or I might get a response that says, "Well, I do not think I understand what you mean." Most of the time a couple does understand what is meant. No matter what they say, I respond with, "How do you feel about that level of involvement?"

These questions are not an attempt to pry and probe into a very personal area of their life. I am really not trying to be voyeuristic in any way, but I am concerned about the extent of the physical relationship for a very sound reason. If the couple has built their relationship upon a physical basis only, they are asking for difficulties later on in the marriage. And if they have gone too far, or further than their standards permit, they might have feelings of guilt, fear, resentment, or even hostility.

In counseling it is important to have the atmosphere and opportunity in which to explore the physical relationship. From time to time a couple sits there, and then one of them might venture to say, "Well, I think we've gone a little further than we really wanted." And then I can say, "Well, could you be more specific for me? Are you saying that you were involved in light petting or heavy petting, or have you been sleeping with one another?" The attitude depends upon the couple. Some couples feel bothered, upset, and guilty if they have been involved in petting. Other couples are bothered only when they have been going to bed together.

I explore further by asking, "Can you tell me some of the feelings that you've had about the extent of your physical relationship? Are you satisfied with it? Have there been problems? What attitudes do you have?" If they have been engaging in sexual intercourse together—and I do run into Christian couples, born-again people who have been involved in sexual relations—I simply share with them part of my beliefs. I tell them that I believe it is very important at that particular time for them to stop having complete sexual relations for two basic reasons. One reason is to find out if their relationship is built on something other than just the physical; refraining from intercourse will really help them to make that decision.

The second major reason for asking them to stop having sexual relations is based on Scripture. The New Testament teaches that we are not to engage in premarital relations. The Scripture calls that fornication. Scriptural teaching should be discussed thoroughly with the couple. (See Appendix for an overview of that teaching.)

So far I have not encountered a couple who has refused to follow this guideline, though from time to time you might find one. The pastor of a large church in southern California follows this particular principle. On many occasions, directly from the pulpit, he has stated this principle which he holds for premarital counseling. He also states that if a couple is not willing to refrain from premarital intercourse, he will not agree to continue the counseling nor to perform the ceremony. That is basically my feeling too. If a couple will not follow that guideline, then the counseling ought to stop.

It is very important for a couple to go into marriage with the proper attitudes and proper behavior. If they have been involved in premarital intercourse, there should be a discussion of their feelings. There should be confession of sin with one another and a time of forgiveness and prayer.

One area that must be considered as one talks about sex is whether or not the young woman is pregnant. If she is pregnant, then various alternatives must be considered. Marriage might not be the best one.

If pregnancy is the main motivation for marriage, it is not sufficient. If the couple is mature, deeply committed to one another, and willing to wait to complete the counseling, and if they realize the adjustments that will be necessary, then marriage could occur. Many couples, however, feel pressured to marry by parents, friends, their own guilt, and even the church.

Other alternatives would be not marrying and either giving up the child for adoption, or, in some cases, keeping the child. The number of abortions each year is increasing steadily; there are many different views regarding that procedure. Pastors differ greatly in their attitudes. My own personal stance is that abortion is not an alternative; if the subject arises, I advise against it. One of the best preventives against abortion in churches and even in secular schools would be the presentation of the outstanding film, *First Days of Life* produced by For Life, Inc., 1917 Xerxes Avenue North, Minneapolis, MN 55411. This film depicts the development of the child from conception to birth. With the use of

X-ray film it shows the fetus in various stages of development.

The sixth area considered in the first session is the extent of their preparation for marriage. You may ask, What preparation have you had for marriage? Have you been reading any books? If so, what books have you read? Have you taken any classes in church or in college, and did you have the classes separately or together? It is necessary to find out what preparation they have had, because some might have been good and some might have been poor.

Another major area to explore is: How have your attitudes toward marriage been influenced, and who influenced them? Quite often parents and brothers and sisters will have had a part in this. The young couple may also have friends who have been married for some time and who provide a model of a good marriage relationship. The "Family History Analysis" is helpful in exploring that particular area.

You will find some couples that have come out of very poor backgrounds with tremendous hostilities, fighting, and multiple divorces within a home; either the man or the woman might have suffered sexual abuse as a young child, and as a result has some problems with his feelings and attitudes in the area of sex. You need to explore and talk with the couple about their background.

Another helpful question has been, What is there about your parents' marriage that you would like in your marriage, and what is there you would not want? After they disclose any trait or characteristic that they do not want ask, How will you avoid this occurring within your marriage? Your parents were models for you, and you have probably incorporated both positive and negative tendencies whether you wanted to or not. What can you do to make sure those traits do not occur in your marriage?

An additional question to ask the couple is: What fears do you have about marriage? Reassure them that most people looking forward to marriage have certain fears, questions, and doubts; you want them to have the opportunity to talk about some of those. You might not get a response; the couple might say, "Well, we really have no fears. We've talked this over and we really think we know all about it." You may want to drop the question at that point. But later on, you will probably discover that they do have some fears. Do not pressure them when they are not ready to discuss their fears; drop the questions for now. You will probably get another chance to help them later.

Another area to discuss is the couple's Christian beliefs. (Some pastors choose to have an extra preliminary interview for this purpose). I do not ask the question, Are you a Christian? It is too easy to respond with, yes, which terminates the conversation. You will learn more by phrasing the question differently. For example, you might ask one of them, "Just tell me a little bit about your own personal spiritual growth and what you believe about the person of Jesus Christ and God." Then sit back and let the person talk.

The majority of the couples that you and I see are born-again believers. But there can be differences between born-again believers. One might be a very strong, growing, maturing Christian. The other may have been a Christian for ten years, but has never really developed any depth in Bible study and prayer, or become particularly involved in the church. If those differences are sensed now, you can begin to work with the couple and help them develop some spiritual growth. That is especially important if the young woman is the one who is very strong as a believer and the man, who is supposed to be the spiritual leader within the marriage relationship, is weak at this time.

Every now and then you will deal with a couple where one is a Christian and the other flatly declares, "No, I'm not a Christian. I do not believe." What do you say at that particular time? If I am counseling such a couple and one partner has shared with me the fact that he or she is not a Christian, I thank him or her for that honesty. Then I take the opportunity to present the gospel and talk about how important spiritual harmony is to a marriage relationship. The unbeliever may then say, "Well, I am really not interested," and that will close the conversation, at least for that particular time. Later on you may have another opportunity to speak of spiritual things.

Do you continue with the premarital counseling when one person remains an unbeliever, or do you stop it? I think it is best to go ahead with the counseling and explain again that you reserve the right to decide whether you will perform the wedding ceremony until later on in the sessions. You can also take the opportunity to explain the teaching of Scripture regarding the marriage of a believer to an unbeliever. The believer may be aware of it and could already have some conflicts over it. Or perhaps he or she is not aware of it. You can point out that the Scripture teaches that a couple is not to be unequally yoked together. You might experience some different reactions at that point: the Christian could be angry or hostile, or he or she might be very agreeable to continuing the premarital counseling.

Pastors who have followed this procedure say they have had varied experiences. A number of the couples have agreed to continue the premarital counseling, realizing that without it the pastor would not agree to perform the ceremony.

What happens in this particular kind of a counseling problem when the non-Christian professes to be a Christian? Would that solve the difficulty? Would you feel like going ahead with the ceremony on the date the couple had planned? It might be best to talk to the couple about postponing the wedding date so the new Christian will have an opportunity to grow in his or her new Christian life. That is important, especially when the new Christian is the young man. A marriage relationship in which the woman is spiritually stronger and more knowledgeable of the Scripture can have problems unless she is very sensitive about her role. You will have many different experiences here.

When a person has accepted the Lord, you could put him or her in contact with other Christians who are involved in Bible study and help them assist the new Christian person in his or her growth. If the new Christian is not concerned about developing his or her spiritual life, that should raise questions as to the genuineness of the decision.

Finally, I like to hear the couple's definition of love. If time has vanished by that point in the discussion, the question may be carried over to the two individual sessions. Each is asked to give his or her definition of love and to answer the question, Why do you believe that you're in love with this particular person?

For a number of years I used to share the following information with the couple. Now most of the time I do not but instead recommend the discussion of the practical meaning of love in the tape series "Enriching Your Marriage."

There are two definitions that I like to suggest to a couple. One is this: "A person is in love with another individual when meeting the emotional needs of that person becomes an emotional need of his or her own life." We discuss and explore that statement to discover what it means in practical daily life.

Another definition is this: "Real love means an unconditional commitment to an imperfect person." That is the love that one needs to have for the person one marries. It is also an illustration of the kind of love that God has toward humanity. His is an unconditional commitment, and all of us are imperfect. If each person realizes that the future mate is imperfect and accepts him or her that way, there is hope!

One young couple I was counseling had an interesting experience. The young woman was delighted about it. She was so happy and jubilant when I saw her that I had to ask, "What are you so happy about?" And she said that about three days before, they were out one evening and her fiancé was just miserable. She said he was stubborn, obstinate, and out-of-sorts. He was really a rat, and yet, in spite of all that, she had the firm conviction that she really loved him. She said, "That was so affirming to me to realize that even at the times when he might be very disagreeable and I might not really like everything he was doing, I'd still have this conviction of love."

An important biblical passage to share is 1 Corinthians 13. I go over it and talk about the ideas it contains, using the *Amplified New Testament.*

Another thing that I discuss with a couple is that in order to really love another person you must love yourself first—you must have a good feeling about yourself. That concept may come up again in connection with the couple's T-JTA scores.

Several other definitions of love may be shared at that point. One is, "Love is a learned emotional reaction." "One does not fall in or out of love; one grows in love."[3] Another is, "Love is not a commodity that can be bartered for, or bought or sold; nor can it be forced upon or from someone. It can only voluntarily be given away."[4] Erich Fromm gave an extensive definition: "Love means to commit oneself without guarantee, to give oneself completely in the hope that our love will produce love in the loved person. Love is an act of faith, and whoever is of little faith is also of little love. The perfect love would be one that gives all and expects nothing. It would, of course, be willing and delighted to take anything it was offered, the more the better. But it would ask for nothing. For if one expects nothing and asks nothing, he can never be deceived or disappointed. It is only when love demands that it brings on pain."[5] That statement sounds very basic and very simple, but it is difficult in practice.

I then ask the couple to share their listings of the indications for marriage and their reasons for marrying the other person. The couple is asked to sit face to face as one shares his list of indications with his fiancé. The lists are to be read in the first person. After that, the partner responds with his list. Then each gives his reasons for marrying the other in the same first-person manner. Here is a listing of one person's indications.

Eight Indications Why This Is the Time to Marry

1. I now have enough experience living alone to know that I prefer not to.
2. I now know that I am able to financially support a wife.
3. However, I expect to be much more secure financially in the relatively near future, and I want to get married before then because I think it can be beneficial to a good relationship to share some minor economic deprivations in the beginning.
4. I may be making my final career decision in the near future, and I would like my wife to be able to share in that decision.
5. I want to leave the Riverside area as soon as practical, and I want to be able to take Mitzi with me.
6. If I am going to have children, I don't want to wait much longer to start having them.
7. I want to go to Europe with my wife while we are both still young enough to enjoy doing it on a very limited budget.
8. But mainly, having made the major decision that getting married will greatly improve my life, I am just naturally eager to start enjoying that improved life-style as soon as possible.

The following is one woman's list of reasons for wanting to marry her fiancé. She entitled this "Why I Want to Marry Jack," and then gave ten reasons: "I love him. He knows and loves Christ as Savior. He is excited about life and wants to accomplish much for God. I want to share and be a part of Jack's life. I want to help Jack become all that God intended him to be. I enjoy being with Jack. We have a good time together. I am physically attracted to him. I can relax and be myself with Jack. I want to care for him, to take care of his home, the meals. He is the kind of man I would want for the father of my children." A person could be quite encouraged by these, for they show a healthy, realistic balance.

Look for a balance as the individuals read their reasons for wanting to marry the other. Occasionally somebody will give reasons like these: I want to marry him because he fulfills all my needs, he takes care of me, he does this for me, he does that for me. The reasons focus on "what the other person can do for me," without the balance of "what I can do for the other person." When a situation like that is encountered, the person should be confronted with what he or she has said.

I remember an occasion when a young lady was listening to her fiancé's reasons for marrying her. The more he read the angrier she became, and before he completed the reasons, she broke in and said, "The reason you want to marry me is for me to do everything for you! What are you going to do for me? Don't you really love me?" The rest of the session was spent talking about the reasons and motivations for their marriage. We were able to settle some of the differences right then and there.

We should be just as concerned, however, when we see an individual giving reasons that indicate that he is going to do everything for the other person. Can that individual accept love? Can he accept the other person's doing something for him? There has to be a balance.

Here is a young man's list of reasons, exactly as he wrote them and shared them in the session:

The Whys and Goals of Our Marriage

The twelve reasons why I'm marrying Betty:

1. The Lord is first in her life. It happened last January, tired of calling her own shots. Consistently has followed that up with a desire to learn, prayer, fellowship, and witnessing.

2. Little girl nature—modest dress, looks young, spontaneity, loves cows, and cute things.

3. Reaches out to other people—senses needs and puts love into action, not just on a one-time basis, but consistent followup. Example—neighbors, friends and work.

4. Responsibility and common sense—Boss said that seldom has he seen a more dedicated person, and one with so much skill in speech therapy. I trust her with maps and directions, to

sometimes handle arrangements where I'm not able. Sets goals and meets them, a budget.

5. She laughs with joy in her heart—she loves pure things, clean and crisp. She wakes up with a smile on her face. She doesn't complain a lot, is willing to roll with the punches. She loves life and wants to reach out and grab it.

6. She cries—she has a depth of feeling for many different situations, work, person who is lost. She uses it to accent her womanhood.

7. She's devoted to our relationship—she's uplifting, encouraging. She speaks the truth in love. She cares what I feel, and respects my desires and interests. She desires to work hard at making it work. She's affectionate and warm.

8. She's intelligent—similar educational background.

9. She sees our relationship as a team ministry. We're walking in the same direction with a common goal, to spread the teaching and life of our Lord Jesus.

10. She's cute (size, shape, face, hair) and clean (neat in appearance, takes care of herself).

11. She's a quick learner. When new things come her way she desires to incorporate them into her life and moves on to the next step.

12. She loves fires, daisies and poems, ie., very romantic, loves beauty, and purity. Enjoys relaxing with the simple things.

13. I love her. I feel good when I'm around her.

Not all lists are so carefully thought out or shared in such detail. By having to write their reasons, couples have been assisted in clarifying and even discovering the specific reasons for marriage. In most instances it has been a delightful experience to observe the nonverbal responses as many are hearing the indications and reasons for the very first time. I have seen several respond with silence and/or tears of delight. Some have decided to incorporate the list of reasons into their wedding vows. The couple is encouraged to keep those lists and share them with one another on their first wedding anniversary.

The "face to face" sitting arrangement is very important. I tell the couple that too often married couples fail to communicate face to face in that manner. They learn to communicate on the run or doing two or three things at the same time. It is vital for intimacy development that couples spend time in uninterrupted face-to-face communication.

Another question that I have asked on occasion is: "What would you like your marriage to become and to reflect?" Some couples will need time to think about that, for it may be a totally new concept. In a way that question can lead them into thinking about goals for their marriage. The word *reflect* could refer back to their own personal, individual qualities or qualities within the relationship. That could be an opportunity to share with them about the spiritual qualities their marriage could reflect.

I next usually ask the couple, "In light of all of the marriages today that are ending in divorce or are unhappy, why will yours be different?" After a brief discussion I show the couple the following chart depicting the level of marital satisfaction over the family life cycle.

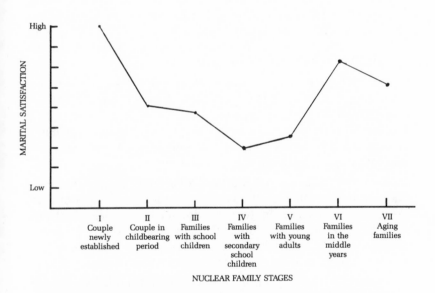

Fig. 1. Husbands' and Wives' Marital Satisfaction over the Family Career. Reprinted from Jane Aldous, *Family Careers—Developmental Change in Families* (New York: John Wiley, 1978), p. 202. Used by permission.

This chart is the result of a number of research studies over the past fifteen years.

Many predictable changes occur as couples proceed through the various stages of the family life cycle. Some of those changes become cripplers of marriage in the process. That occurs because the couple does not anticipate or plan for the events and changes that often occur at each stage.

Often a man builds his identity through his occupation or profession. Many men pursue goals of making a good living and finding a good life, which prove to them they are adequate and of worth. (That typically male process is undergoing some change, however, as many women are now pursuing careers and professions.) Because their identities are built in that manner, men devote their time and energy to their work. The marital relationship often takes a secondary position. When couples marry, the timing is such that most men are just at the point of establishing themselves in their line of work. Their main task at that time is establishing identity through their work. At the onset of marriage a wife is seeking to build an intimate relationship with her husband. That is where frustration may occur. It can be described as identity versus intimacy!

Underlying part of many wives' strong emphasis upon intimacy is their own striving for building their sense of identity. Often a wife builds an identity through her husband or family. (That typically female process is undergoing some change too as many women are now being employed outside of the home and some marital roles are changing.)

Many wives become discouraged after a few years of marriage because the intimate relationship with their husband does not develop as expected. In time a wife may turn her efforts for intimacy toward the children. Perhaps that accounts for many mothers finding it so difficult to let go of the children when they are old enough to leave the nest.

If that situation continues—the husband building identity through work and the wife building intimacy and identity through the children—a crisis will eventually occur. Many husbands in their forties realize they have reached the end of the line for upward progress in their work. There is nowhere else to go, so their goals begin to change. They may now turn back to their wives with a desire to build intimacy. They could be in for a shock, because many wives, after the children leave home, begin to consider how their own identities have developed. They may now decide either to complete their own education or to pursue a career. Their desire for an intimate relationship with their husbands is not very intense after so many years of no reciprocation on his part. The issues of the meaning of achievement and values in relationships needs attention during marital counseling because often they are the underlying cause of the symptomatic problems couples bring to counseling.

I ask the couple to notice the drop in marital satisfaction on the chart during the child-rearing years. Then I ask, "Why does the presence of children affect marital satisfaction so much? Why does the level continue to drop?" We then talk about the idea that that trend, or tendency, on the part of couples does not have to occur. What will they do so that does not happen to them in their marriage?

Flexibility and adaptability are important on the part of the pastor or counselor conducting the premarital sessions. Each couple will vary in their abilities, needs, or problem areas, and the amount of time given to each topic will vary. With a few couples all of this material may be covered during the first session. With most, however, it will carry over into an additional session with the couple together, or you may extend the first session to an hour and a half. Often it has taken more than six sessions to complete the series.

A couple may come with special circumstances that warrant exploration. During the first session with a couple I knew minimally it was apparent that there was some difference in their ages. Upon asking they said that she was twenty-four and he was thirty-eight. The next question was: "Have the two of you had the opportunity to discuss the advantages and disadvantages of the age differences?" The way that a question is posed and constructed is significant. They were not asked, "What are the problems that you see with the age difference?" That could put them on the defensive. Questions should be phrased to enable a couple to think about the situation or area of concern in a new light.

At this point the first homework assignment is given to the couple. This assignment, like the others that follow, is to be completed individually and not discussed between them. The first assignment should be completed before the third session.

At the end of the session I explain about the required books and tapes and help them develop a time schedule for the books. They purchase the books so they will have them to keep, and the tapes are loaned to them. First "Enriching Your Marriage" and then Dr. Wheat's series is listened to. The first book to read is *Communication—Key to Your Marriage*. Then I ask them to answer the following questions in writing before the next session.

1. Write a paragraph on what you are bringing to this marriage that will make it work. (It should deal with what each one has to contribute to the marriage.)

2. Write down your role and the responsibilities that you will have within the marriage; write down what you believe the role and responsibilities of your spouse will be. (Each person is to do this individually, and they are to be very specific and detailed.)

3. What will you get out of marriage that you would not have gotten if you had remained single?

4. If both sets of parents are in favor of the marriage, I give one final assignment, not to the couple but to their parents. I have each person ask his or her parents to write a letter to me telling why they want this young man or woman to become their son- or daughter-in-law. They are not to show this to their son or daughter but to mail it to me. During the last counseling session I read these letters to the couple. This is an affirming time and greatly enhances total family relationships.

In addition to this question, each parent (both mother and father) is given a copy of the in-law evaluation form, and they are asked to complete it and return it to the pastor. This will be given to the couple, and they will probably want to respond to their parents' response. As you can see from the questions, the purpose of this questionnaire is two-fold: to build positive concern and communication between the parents and future in-laws and again to help eliminate potential problems that could occur.

Becoming An In-law—Building Positive Relationships

1. How would you describe your relationship with your parents and in-laws during the early years of your marriage?

Parents: _____

_____

In-laws: _____

_____

2. Would you like your married children to approach you in the same way you approached your parents and in-laws? Why or why not? _____

3. What would you list as some major needs of your soon-to-be married son or daughter? Could those needs be best met (1) with your help, (2) by himself or herself, or (3) with the new marriage partner? _____

4. Are there some unique needs of your mate related to the leaving of your child? How might you help him or her in these areas? _____

5. What will be the greatest adjustment that you will have to make as your son or daughter leaves home? _____

6. If you could ask your son or daugther to pray for you as you make this transition, what would you ask them to pray? _____

7. Will you expect the new couple to visit you often? How do you define "often?" How will you go about suggesting they visit you? _____

8. When the newlyweds choose something that is not your choice, what do you think your response will be? (Can you think of an example?) _____

9. Do you expect the newly married couple to call before visiting you and vice versa? Can there be spontaneous "drop ins"? _____

10. What plans, secrets, and problems do you expect the new couple to share with you? If that does not happen, what do you think your reaction will be? _____

_____

11. In what way do you think and speak of your son- or daughter-in-law as a positive addition to your family? _____

_____

_____

12. In what way are you taking into consideration the feelings of the other family (parents-in-law) in making wedding plans? ____

Scheduling holiday visits? _____

Giving gifts? _____
Seeing the grandchildren? _____

13. Please describe six expectations that you have for the couple after they are married. _____

_____

_____

_____

14. Please take another piece of paper and together compose a letter describing in detail why you are looking forward to your son's or daughter's fiancé becoming your son- or daughter-in-law. This should be addressed to that person. Please write at least three paragraphs. _____

_____

At that time it is important to give the assignments for the remainder of the sessions from the *Before You Say I Do* workbook. Many pastors have all the assignments and other questions printed off so they can be handed to the couple.

Some of the assignments from *Before You Say I Do* will be discussed during the sessions, and some will not. That is a decision that each pastor needs to make, and it could be based upon the maturity of the couple and what you believe each couple needs to cover with you. Remember that each person is to have his/her own copy of the workbook. Here is a suggested schedule that I use with couples although it will vary:

- *To be completed by the second session*
  Chapter 1—What is marriage?
  Chapter 2—Uniqueness and acceptance in marriage
- *To be completed by the third session*
  Chapter 4—What do you expect from marriage?
  Chapter 5—Goals in marriage

- *To be completed by the fourth session*
  Chapter 6—Fulfilling needs in marriage
  Chapter 7—Roles, responsibilities and decision-making
- *To be completed by the fifth session*
  Chapter 9—Communication
  Chapter 10—Conflict
  Chapter 11—Finances (Often I prefer to discuss some of chapter 10 with the couple prior to their working through the chapter together.)
  Chapter 3—"Love as a basis for marriage" is often suggested as a Bible study for the couple to complete while on their honeymoon.

It is often helpful to conclude each session with a significant idea or illustration. The following has given insight to many couples:

> You must work at your marriage both to give it life and to keep it vigorous. Divorce is not the only thing that will kill a marriage.
>
> Indifference will kill a marriage. Neglect will kill a marriage. Drifting apart and separating in interests and associations will kill a marriage. I once came across the story of a childless couple whose marriage had been in a state of living death for many years. Nevertheless, for reasons convincing to themselves, they wished to avoid a legal separation. Instead, for years they went their separate ways, maintaining separate bedrooms, eating breakfast and lunch separately and engaging in separate activities during the day. If they met at the dinner table or for social engagements, it was generally in the presence of friends. They avoided being alone with each other.
>
> One day, the husband, who was a very prominent citizen, learned from some friends that his wife had written a book which was becoming a literary success. He read it and discovered it was autobiographical. Its contents contained a suspicion of scandal. It told of the author's heartbreak in the loss of a man whom she had lived with many years ago and who now was gone forever. The date of her deep interest in this man with whom she had lived as revealed in the book was after they had been married. The husband angrily confronted his wife and charged her with adultery. He demanded to know the name of her secret lover. For a long time she refused to tell him. At length, she cried: "You were that man. You were once the wonderful, idealistic young man whom I loved and adored. But that man died long ago. Now all I have left is the

man he became—one whom I know to be selfish, mean and a cheat, one whom I can no longer love or respect."[6]

For the second session you will see each person separately, so you really have two meetings. This is the time when I show each person the results of the "Taylor-Johnson Temperament Analysis." As mentioned, they were asked to complete the tests at home without discussing them with one another and to send them back before the first session. The tests are ready when they come in for individual sessions.

I explore with the person the results of the test that he answered regarding himself, and the results of his answers regarding his fiancé. I do not show the results of the other person's answers regarding himself or the fiancé. These I hold until the session when they come together. For now they can see their own score and the score reflecting the way they saw the other person. We might spend ten or twenty minutes on this, or we might spend the entire session. I have found that some people need several private counseling sessions because of information discovered through the T-JTA.

The test is very helpful in uncovering problem areas or potential problem areas that could erupt within the marriage. As you look at a person's profile, you may discover that he has a very high score in nervousness, or depressiveness, or one may be too submissive. Another may be too subjective, or too hostile, or very, very impulsive. All those could contribute to difficulties within the marriage relationship. We look not only at the profile reflecting the person's view of himself, but also at the profile reflecting his view of his fiancé.

There are occasions when I may choose to see the couple together for most of the second session. That is done if the couple is very emotionally mature, or if it appears that sharing the results together would enhance the discussion and communication process. Part of the session, though, needs to be separate so each has the opportunity for individual interaction with you.

After going over the T-JTA scores, I ask some of the same questions that I have asked when two of them were together in the first session. You may wonder, "Why do you do this?" One reason is that I often get different answers the second time around. If a person is hesitant about revealing some of his or her fears, anxieties, or guilt over sexual behavior, this provides an opportunity to share those without the presence of the other person. And so I do ask some of the same questions, especially if I have been somewhat suspicious or concerned about the answers received during the initial interview.

One couple who had been engaged in heavy petting both told me in the first session, "It really doesn't bother us." But when we started the individual session the young lady said, "I wanted to bring up something we discussed in the first interview. I really have felt very badly about the sexual behavior, and I didn't know how to discuss this with my fiancé. I didn't want to hurt his feelings, and I didn't want to get into an argument, because I feel he is much more dominant than I am. What can I do about this?" So we discussed her feelings. Actually I felt that she wanted me to tell her fiancé that she did not like the sexual behavior. My response was that if I did this I would be assuming a responsibility that was not mine. So I spent time helping her to formulate how she would share this with her fiancé. And she was able to do so.

Sometimes a couple will choose to discuss their feelings further on the outside when I am not present. On other occasions they wait until I am there so that all three of us can be involved in the discussion.

After going over some of these repeat questions, we spend time on any problems that the person anticipates in the marriage. Topics vary from individual differences to in-laws, where they're going to live, schooling, and finances. Again I make it clear that there is nothing that the person cannot ask me or bring up.

Finally, we discuss the question that I asked the person to answer in preparation for the session: What do you think that you are going to get out of marriage that you would not get if you were to remain single? That question has provoked quite a bit of discussion and response, not only when it is asked of an individual, but in groups of married couples.

Each session with an individual will be different. With one person you might concentrate on topics that do not even come up with another person. Usually the session takes a good hour, sometimes even more; and again, as mentioned earlier, if there are some difficulties revealed by the Taylor-Johnson test, you might have to arrange for additional individual sessions ministering to that person.

SUGGESTED OUTLINE FOR SESSION ONE

Getting Acquainted

(Note: Session One should either be one 1½ hour session or 2 one-hour sessions to cover this content.)

1. Pastor shares information about himself such as background, family, hobbies, schools, and some of his interesting experiences in marriage.
2. Lay ground rules: (a) There is nothing that cannot be discussed in these sessions; (b) the couple must complete their outside assignments if the counseling is to continue.

Marriage Defined

1. What are their expectations for the premarital period?
2. Ask couple why they are coming to the church to be married instead of going to a justice of the peace. Why is the church important?
3. Ask couple to share their definition of marriage.
4. Pastor shares definitions given in this chapter.

Family Backgrounds—Use the information from the "Family History Analysis."

1. Have the couple share something about their homes and families, such as where they lived, in what type of home, what their parents did, are they still together, whether they have brothers and sisters, their position, and what type of relationships they have, the financial status of the home, whether the family moved around or lived in one place. Is there any dependency remaining upon their parents?
2. Ask how did their parents' physical and mental health relate to them in growing up? How did their parents handle disagreements? Which parents did each admire the most?
3. How were feelings of love, warmth, and tenderness shown in their homes as they were growing up?
4. How would they like to have feelings of love, warmth, and tenderness shown to them in public and in their home?

5. What differences do they see between themselves? Are these differences sources of potential problems? What can they do to solve the problems?

Dating Background

1. How long have they been going together? What kind of dates have they had? What have they done on their dates and where have they gone? Have they included other friends or have they just dated together?
2. Have they had opportunities to become acquainted with each other's parents?
3. Discuss their courtship and how it will contribute to their marital relationship.

Sexual Understanding

1. Who prepared them in terms of their understanding about sex? Who talked with them? What books have they read?
2. Most couples desire to express their affection in some physical manner. To what extent have they expressed their affection to one another?
3. Can they tell you some of the feelings that they've had about the extent of their physical relationship? Are they satisfied with it? Have there been problems? What attitudes do they have?
4. (If applicable) Is the woman pregnant?

Preparation for Marriage

1. What preparation have they had for marriage? Have they been reading any books? If so, what books have they read? Have they taken any classes in church or in college, and did they have the classes separately or together?

Attitudes Toward Marriage

1. Who has influenced their attitudes toward marriage, and how have the attitudes been influenced?
2. What fears do they have concerning marriage?
3. What do they want and not want from their parents' marriages?

Spiritual Maturity

1. Ask them about their spiritual growth and what they believe about the Person of Jesus Christ and God.

Love Defined

1. Ask each one why he believes he's in love with that particular person.

Indications and Reasons

1. Ask the couple to sit face to face and share their list of indications and reasons.

The Future of Their Marriage

1. What would you like your marriage to become and reflect?
2. In light of all of the marriages today that are ending in divorce or are unhappy, why will yours be different?
3. Discussion of the chart "Marital Satisfaction."

Homework Assignment

1. Assign questions to be answered before the third counseling session.
2. Explain any other tests you want them to take.
3. Conclude with quote, page 110.

SUGGESTED OUTLINE FOR SESSION TWO

Taylor-Johnson test

1. Explore the results of the test.
2. Answer questions.

Anticipation of Marriage

1. Ask what problems they anticipate in their marriage.
2. Ask what do they think they will get out of marriage that they would not get if they remained single.

NOTES

1. David Augsburger, *Cherishable: Love and Marriage* (Scottdale, Pa.: Herald Press, 1971), p. 16.
2. David Hubbard, president of Fuller Theological Seminary, in an address.
3. Leo Buscaglia, *Love* (Thorofare, N.J.: Slack, 1972), pp. 61-62.
4. Ibid., p. 63.
5. Quoted in Buscaglia, p. 66.
6. Louis Binstock, *The Power of Maturity* (New York: Hawthorn, 1969), pp. 104-5.

6

The Third and Fourth Sessions

The content of the third and fourth sessions in premarital counseling is listed together because it is difficult to know how much will be covered in the third session. In some cases much of this material will be covered; in others, most of the time will be spent talking about the "Taylor-Johnson Temperament Analysis." As you work with different couples you will find that with some you will need three sessions to cover all this material; with others you will be able to cover it very comfortably in two sessions.

When the couple arrives for the third session they are usually very interested in looking at the Taylor-Johnson test. They have seen their own profile and how they perceive the other person, but they have not seen the other's profile nor how their fiancé perceives them. The discussion centers upon the test. You might start by showing the man's profile to the woman and discussing potential problems, then show the woman's to the man. Finally, show them how they see one another. Usually they will have a number of questions.

A typical situation may be that of a young man who scores himself very high on sympathy; when he sees that his fiancée scored him very low, he wants to know, "Why do you see me like that? I am a very loving and caring individual." Perhaps he is, but he might not be sharing this with her or verbalizing it so that she perceives it.

It is important to focus on the personality differences, the areas of possible adjustment. I like to focus on how the two people are alike and how they are different. You are not looking for a couple to have identical profiles. There are very, very few who are identical in their T-JTA profile. In fact, some who are too much alike may have difficulties. Maybe the man and the woman both score ninety-five on the dominant scale. Look at one of the Taylor-Johnson profiles now and you will see what the potential problem might be with the couple. Two individuals who are very dominant may be headed for trouble if they do not learn to ease off, to give, and to adjust to the other person.

At this time it is helpful to ask, In what way are your parents like you? How are you like them? Which of the traits or qualities of your parents are you looking for in your spouse? We discuss how the personalities of the parents may have influenced the young people. It is helpful to discuss how this might carry over into the marriage relationship.

It is difficult to know how long it will take to cover the T-JTA. If there are problem areas evident, I give specific assignments which must be completed during the time of the premarital counseling. See the Appendix for books and tapes which can be used with the T-JTA. After the discussion of the T-JTA, we might spend time discussing the "Marriage Prediction Schedule," particularly if it has uncovered some extremes and noticeable differences.

Next we discuss the assignments and questions given as homework. Those were: (1) write a paragraph on what you are bringing to this marriage that will make the marriage work; (2) write out your own role and responsibility and the role and responsibility of your spouse; and (3) answer the question, What will you get out of marriage that you wouldn't get if you remained single?

Here is a paragraph that a young woman wrote in response to the question concerning her role:

My Role

As his wife, I should be a companion and a friend. I must support and encourage him in spiritual growth and his daily work. I should be someone he can share with and find acceptance, security and love no matter what mistakes he has made. I have the responsibility and joy of meeting his physical needs. My role as wife is submissive in the sense that God has given him primary responsibility in our relationship. The final decisions do not rest with me. My job is to create an environment where he and our children can become all that God intended them to be.

I find that most couples do not go into sufficient detail in the area of roles. The resource found on page 41 of *Before You Say I Do*—"Your Role Concepts Comparison Sheet"—has been helpful. There may be times when you ask the couple to turn to that section and discuss some of the questions even though this assignment from the workbook is for a later session.

Each question may be answered in one of five ways: agree, strongly agree, mildly agree, or strongly disagree. The partners answer without looking at one another's copy.

Note that the second question states, "The wife should not be employed outside of the home." You might find one person who is not sure and one who strongly agrees or disagrees. It is important to stop at this time and talk about this area to see why they have differences of opinion and how this is going to affect their marriage relationship.

Looking down the sheet, you find other questions that might bring up discussion. For example, "The husband should babysit one night a week so the wife can get away and do what she wants," or, "A couple should spend their recreational and leisure time together," or, "It is all right for the wife to initiate love-making with her husband." If you find differences of opinion here, then you need to discuss these.

One of the areas of concern that will arise is the question of "Should the wife work?" A couple of questions on the sheet relate to that area, and you need to explore some of the particular problems that might arise if she works. However, you must also allow the freedom for the couple to make the final decision.

You may have a man who is very adamant against his wife working, yet his fiancée is a college graduate and has a profession. She has spent years training for her position and feels that it is very important for her to be able to continue in it. This is where you have to explore some of the reasons behind each person's attitude as well as work toward some type of reconciliation of the two conflicting opinions. One personal conviction that I try to get across is that it's very important when children are in the preschool years for the mother to be the one who is responsible for training, guiding them, and nurturing them. After the children are old enough to go to school, then the wife might find it beneficial to be employed.

With the changing economic conditions more and more women will be employed, and some of our traditional life-styles will be modified. Her salary, though, should not be used just for her own needs, but for the entire family. However, there will be exceptions. You may want to share some practical principles to follow if a wife is going to work. Some helpful material is found in the Appendix of this book titled "Husband-Wife Roles in the Twentieth Century."

One of the finest books clarifying husband/wife roles from a biblical perspective is *Marriage as Equal Partnership* by Dwight H. Small (Grand Rapids: Baker, 1980).

Another "homework" question that is discussed is, "What are you bringing to this marriage that will make it work?" One woman wrote:

> I am bringing a love for Jack and a desire to meet his needs. I am aware of his strengths and his weaknesses. I realize the importance of unselfish giving and feel, for the most part, I am capable of that. I have common sense, intelligence, and leadership abilities that are important in caring for a home and a family. I am not governed by emotions and I usually am willing to express and talk about problems. I have a forgiving spirit and a sense of humor.

Here is one written by a young man as he came in to the premarital counseling session.

> I believe that I am bringing much to marriage that will help it to be successful. My faith in Christ is the greatest single element that will make our marriage successful. I believe beyond all doubt that God designed for us to be joined in marriage. I have abilities in leadership that will allow me to carry out my role as head of my house. I have confidence that I can carry the responsibility of marriage. I am willing to sacrifice things that I want for the attainment of the highest good. I have an understanding of what God intended a marriage to be. I have tremendous determination to make my marriage successful above all else. I see marriage as a top priority. I have an ability to sense the needs of others, and I have strengths in being able to listen to people.

Here you have two examples of what people feel they are bringing to a marriage relationship that will make it work. Of course, people's comments are not always of this quality. Some are lacking; their reasons for marriage might be very immature. I can remember one person who wrote, "He makes me feel good all the time. He causes me to laugh. I feel fun with him." It was very superficial. When people's comments are of this nature, we need to discuss their ideas and the realities of marriage in depth. If one's reasons for marriage are superficial—looks, youth—those reasons might disappear; then what is left of the marriage relationship?

There are several more questions that I like to ask at this time to direct the couple's thinking deeper. The first is: "Name the personal characteristics that you possess that will build up a marriage. Name the personal characteristics your partner possesses that might tend to tear down the marriage." I have the couple write down their answers; then we share them. By this time the couple is quite perceptive, with a real freedom to discuss and share.

The next question elicits some surprise: "How are you going to change your mate?" Sometimes they look back as though to say, "What do you mean, 'change my mate'? He's perfect the way he is." You might have to reemphasize this by saying, "Well, most people do find some behavior or attitudes in their fiancé or their spouse that irritate or bother them, and they might want to change them. Now, how are you going to go about changing this person?" Or, better yet, "What have you already done to change the person?" The person might share, "I don't want to change her. She's exactly as I like her." This might be very true and very honest for now. On the other hand, some people who appear to have this attitude are actually thinking, "After I get married, I'm going to start modifying him."

It is unfortunate when one attempts to turn the other person into a revised edition of himself. In marriage counseling, I sometimes encounter a spouse who will say, "You know, the thing that attracted me to this individual when we were dating and when we were engaged is the very thing that I'm trying so desperately to change right now. I liked it to begin with, but now I am trying to change it." I may ask, "Are you being successful?"

More often than not the response is, "Why, no, that's why I'm here. It isn't working."

As we look at this matter of attempting to change one's mate, we start exploring some of the attitudes and ideas that the two people might have toward each other. Basically what I want to get across to them is a statement presented by Cecil Osborne in *The Art of Understanding Your Mate*. He suggests a way in which you can change your spouse. To summarize it, if you really want to change the person that you're married to, you change yourself. The other person will change in response to the changes that he or she sees in your life. But if your goal is trying to modify or change the other person, it is not going to work. We have to begin with ourselves.

A friend told me that for years and years he kept praying that God would change his wife and change his children. And for some reason God did not seem to answer him in the way he wanted, and his wife and children did not change. Then one day he started praying in a very different way. He said, "Lord, change my life. Change me, mold me into the kind of man and husband and father I need to be." Then the man said, "You know, the strangest thing happened. My wife and my children changed." They changed because he changed.

If young married people would work on needed changes in their own lives, then the partner's defects and problems would not seem as large. Naturally, most couples do find areas that concern them. It is unrealistic to think that a person will be totally accepting. Some faults or behavior ought to be altered. A couple needs the freedom to express their concerns and irritations to one another, but they cannot force one another to change. All they can do is to bring problems to the other's awareness, then leave it up to the other to respond as he or she sees fit.

Two additional principles of changing one's spouse could be pointed out to the couple. One concerns complaints. When most individuals make a complaint it is done in a negative and general manner. An example would be "You're never affectionate." That is likely to generate a defensive response. Reversing it is more likely to bring about a positive response. Complaints should be positive and specific; in other words, point to the desired behavior that you would like to see rather than focusing upon the problem. A statement like "I would appreciate it if you would touch me and hold me some each day" stated in a positive loving tone of voice is more likely to bring a positive response.

Another point to share with the couple is the fact that when a person wants to eliminate an undesirable behavior in his spouse he usually goes about it in such a way that he reinforces the behavior he does not like. I ask the couple for examples or ways in which that occurs and usually they are aware of the problem.

It is helpful to ask about their response to the homework assignments from *Before You Say I Do*, especially chapter 4, "*Expectations*," and chapter 5, "*Goals*." Those chapters are essential for they help eliminate some of the conflicting surprises from marriage and help to give direction to the marriage.

The homework project on expectations, which the couple completed, is the following as described in *Before You Say I Do*.

> The next exercise will take some thought and time on your part. Write twenty expectations you will have of your fiancé when you are married. They can be simple or elaborate. For example, a husband might expect his wife to be at the door when he arrives home, always to be at home and never work, and to have sex with him whenever he wants it. A wife might expect her husband to go to her parents' house with her whenever she goes, to be the spiritual leader in their home, and to spend Saturdays at home and not out hunting.
>
> Now let's go back to your twenty expectations of your future spouse. Take each expectation and, on a separate piece of paper, write one or two sentences indicating how your marriage relationship would be affected if this expectation were not met.
>
> Now, take your list of twenty expectations and share your list with your fiancé. Take your fiancé's list and read it to yourself. As you read each one of your fiancé's expectations of you, place a check mark under the appropriate column. C stands for "cinch." You feel that the expectation you have just read is going to be a "cinch" to fulfill. S stands for "sweat." It will take some hard work and sweat but it can be done. N stands for "no way." You feel that the expectation is impossible. When the two of you have completed your evaluation of the expectations, give them back and then spend some time discussing them.[1]

Many surprises emerge from this exercise and it has proved to be one of the most helpful.

The next question to consider is the goals that they have for their marriage relationship. Here are some goals that were brought in by a young woman. These are just as she expressed them:

First of all, to encourage the spiritual growth of each person. To encourage the physical, mental, and emotional growth of the other person. To produce an environment and relationship that reflects God's love to others. To raise children who know and love God and are equipped to live in society. To produce a relationship and home that is full of joy and excitement. To have a relationship where the basic needs of each person can be met in the other.

Now notice the difference between this list and the next one. The goals of the following list are much more specific, time related, and measurable. (For more information on marital goals see H. Norman Wright, *The Pillars of Marriage* from Regal Books, 1979).

Eight Goals for Marriage Relationship

1. Make the first four minutes together (morning, evening, and so on) quality time of building and affirming daily affection.
2. Pray together on our knees in a good-sized prayer session (10-15 min.) once weekly, and pray together daily (not just meals).
3. Study the Bible together once a week besides individual quiet times and/or reading Scripture at supper.
4. Refine communication patterns so that we go to sleep only after both partners are satisfied that they are understood and accepted by the other, and all is forgiven.
5. Practice hospitality. Have kids or a couple of friends over for a meal twice a month.
6. Get feedback on how marriage is going once a month. Take a two- to three-hour block and discuss growth and satisfactions as well as dissatisfaction and "unimportant things."
7. Strive for sexual patterns that are creative, satisfying, and exciting to both partners most of the time; understanding of partner's moods, and so on.
8. Seek to use each other as our best critics; seek constructive criticism from each other and be able to give it.

One of the questions to explore at this time is, What are you going to do to meet these goals or to reach them? You can determine how detailed a plan the individual or the couple has worked out to achieve their mutual goals. If they need help, you can assist them in the process.

Now you may want to spend some time getting the couple's reactions to the reading material. By now they should have completed their individual books and the book by Ed and Gail Wheat, *Intended for Pleasure.*

Sometimes when you ask, "What do you think of the material you're reading?" One person may say, "I really didn't like it. It didn't help me at all. I don't see why you asked me to read it." This is a time when you need to be careful and refrain from being defensive. Simply ask the person to elaborate: "Well, can you tell me more about that? What are some of the things you didn't like?" This leads into a discussion, and perhaps you will see that the reading was hitting too close to home. The person may have seen himself in some of the cases mentioned. Or he found some problems brought out in his life for the first time and did not know how to handle them.

It is helpful to get feedback concerning the books; it also serves as a reminder to the couple that they need to keep up on their reading. I require a couple to complete all the reading before we have finished premarital counseling.

Now we spend some time talking about sex, the honeymoon, and children. Attitudes expressed earlier may indicate that it is essential to spend some time talking in this area. It is helpful to talk with the couple about the way in which the Scriptures present the subject of sex. God created sex, and it is to be used for several specific purposes. Procreation is not the only purpose of sex; sex is also meant for pleasure; it is a means of relating to one another and being close to one another; it is a time of giving to each other.

We also need to talk about specific details, because sometimes couples make mistakes as they go into the sexual relationship. Quite often the woman has heard quite a bit of discussion about the question, "Do women really have orgasms?" They might have misconceptions. The series of tapes by Dr. Wheat helps reduce the time spent in counseling in this area. They answer many questions ahead of time. The book by the Wheats should also help.

Encourage the couple to be able to talk together freely about sex. One of the factors that contributes to a healthy sexual relationship is the ability to talk about what they are doing when they are doing it. If something is not pleasing to one, he or she should say so. If one is not comfortable, he or she should express it. I also point out that if one person is having difficulty adjusting sexually, it might not be just his or her own fault or responsibility, but a matter of both partners working together. There is a kind of tuning process that has to occur as each individual comes to know what the other person's body is like and how they relate together.

Additional books may be helpful. One is *The Key to Feminine Response in Marriage* by Ronald Deutsch, which gives specific guidelines concerning what an orgasm is actually like and how the husband can assist his wife in coming to a complete climax. Another recent and thought-provoking book is *The Joy of Being a Woman* written by Ingrid Trobisch, Harper & Row.

I tell the couple that there is no set time or set place in the house where the sexual relationship must occur. They need flexibility and freedom about time and place. They also need to be made aware of the importance of cleanliness; taking a shower or a bath is very important because the nose is so sensitive to odors. Odor can either excite an individual or actually inhibit excitement.

It is necessary to talk frankly and directly to the man, because men sometimes have a tendency to be insensitive to some of the little things that are important to a woman, especially the idea of showing her affection at all times during the day. A man should give his wife frequent hugs and kisses without each one having to lead to the bedroom. Some women have complained that the only time their husbands expressed affection to them was when they wanted intercourse. Affection and attention should occur every day whether intercourse is intended or not. Often couples rush around all day at a frantic pace, and then all of a sudden they arrive in the bedroom. They're exhausted, but they feel, "Well, now's the time that we have to express our love toward one another sexually," and they do not achieve the satisfaction they ought to be achieving. Timing and sensitivity are basic.

It is also basic procedure that both individuals should have thorough physical exams by their medical doctor before the wedding. In most states certain blood tests have to be performed before a couple can obtain a marriage license. If neither party has a doctor or knows of one in the area, I give them a list of several names. The tape series by Dr. Wheat discusses methods of contraception; encourage the couple to continue this discussion with their doctor.

When it comes to the honeymoon, there are several suggestions to make concerning sexual behavior. Some couples seem to be convinced that intercourse is mandatory on the wedding night. But this could be the worst time if the couple has had a busy day, an eight o'clock wedding, a reception at the church, another reception at the parents' home afterwards, the get-away at one o'clock in the morning, a drive of a hundred miles, and the arrival at a strange motel at two or three in the morning. The couple is exhausted physically and emotionally, but then they feel, "We must have relations." Often it is a disappointment for both. If they are going to be very busy and going to have a late wedding, I suggest that they just get some sleep, and when they awake in the morning, they will have plenty of time, they will be relaxed and have their strength back, and they can have an experience that will be very beautiful. We must also caution them against expecting too much from the sexual relationship, especially if it is the first time. Most couples learn to respond to one another; the satisfaction and enjoyment they derive from the sexual relationship ten years later is generally much better than the initial encounter.

Tell them a sense of humor helps, because both of them could make some mistakes. They may feel uncomfortable, awkward, slightly embarrassed, and not know exactly what to do. We have heard of situations where the bed has collapsed or somebody has fallen out of bed, or there's a short in the wiring in the building and suddenly the lights come on. These are shocking events, but a sense of humor will help the couple work toward a healthy adjustment.

Now is a good time to discuss how many children the couple would like to have, and when they plan to have children. Even though they do not have children at this point (at least, most of the couples we see do not have children), this is an opportunity to talk with them about the importance of being united in their principles for disciplining and rearing their children. Two or three books could be suggested to them at this time. One book I have found very helpful is *Help! I'm a Parent* (Zondervan, 1979) by Dr. S. Bruce Narramore. A workbook accompanies this volume. I suggest that they read and discuss the book and work through the workbook before they have children.

I also suggest that when it comes time for them to consider

having a family, one of the best educational experiences they could have to prepare themselves for children would be to volunteer to work in either the nursery department or the toddler department of their church. They should work as a team, teaching and helping the children for six to ten months. They will become better acquainted with what children are like and have a better idea of what to expect when their own children come along.

I encourage the couple to be sure to read *Preparing for Parenthood* by Marvin N. Inmon and H. Norman Wright, (Ventura, Cal.: Regal, 1980).

Ask the couple how many years of their married life they want to give to rearing children. Most have never considered this. The following formula can be shared with them to help them discover the realities of parenthood.

_____Number of children desired.

$\times$ _____Years apart you want your children.

$=$ _____Total

$+$ _____Add 18 years

$=$ _____Total years you will be raising a family.

$+$ _____Age when you will have your first child.

$=$ _____Your age when you will be free as a couple again and the children are grown.

From time to time a pastor finds himself counseling people who present an unusual set of circumstances. One such couple that I counseled arrived for the session together. The woman was twenty-eight years of age and had been married before. Her previous husband had been on drugs, had been involved with several other women, and had deserted the family. There was one child, who was about eight or nine. The woman was on welfare because of the lack of support from her previous husband. She was a born-again Christian.

The man was forty and had never been married. He had not had any real dating experience before meeting this woman, but they had been dating now for about a year and a half, and seemed to be very much in love. She was about four or five inches taller than he and other differences were apparent in terms of their personality makeup. What would be your response to this couple? What areas of adjustment would you focus on? And what are some of the questions you might ask them?

I explored several areas with these two individuals. The woman had been living on her own for some time and had assumed the role and responsibility of both mother and father. She had been required to take responsibility for all areas of the home. Would she be willing to give up appropriate areas to her new husband? They had already discussed this and worked out a solution.

Another potential problem was that he had not dated much and had waited until he was almost forty before deciding to get married. What was the reason for this? He just had not found the woman God wanted him to marry.

Another area of concern was the difference in their stature. We discussed it; both of them felt very comfortable about it.

Was this man going to be able to adjust to the woman's eight-year-old daughter? One of the positive elements in the relationship was related to his employment: he had been an elementary school physical education teacher for eighteen years. He knew what elementary-age children were like and had worked with them; in fact, he had already assumed some of the role of helping to discipline within the home. This had already been worked out, and the woman's daughter felt very positively about this man. There were differences and yet they were aware of them and were working on them.

Another factor had to be considered: Would he be aware of what it was going to cost to care for a family? We discussed in detail some of the new expenses he would be having in this family life. In a case like this it would be helpful for the man to shop with the woman in a department store and discover the cost of women's and children's clothing.

All in all, this couple was a delight to counsel. They were both genuine Christians; the person of Christ seemed to be at the center of their relationship. They had already made a positive adjustment.

In-laws are a topic for discussion. Unfortunately, over the years in-laws have been the brunt of so many jokes that we assume that a couple will experience difficulty with them. It is important to explore a couple's feelings about and relationships with both sets of parents. Many questions can be asked here. What is each one's attitude toward their parents and their fiancé's parents? Much of this may have been discussed already. We ask, "How close are you going to live to them?" Do you feel that it would be possible for you to live a thousand miles away from your own parents?" If a couple or individual is incapable of living far away from their own parents, they might not be ready for marriage. Genesis 2:24 states, A person shall "leave" his parents and "cleave" to his wife. The word leave in the Hebrew actually means "to abandon, to forsake, to cut off, to sever a relationship before you start a new one." Those words are used in a positive sense and do not mean alienation of family members. But it is important to realize that some people may leave home physically but not emotionally. Perhaps the idea of living that far away can assist us in determining whether the person can really make that separation from the parents.

Parents and children need to say good-bye to one another when a marriage occurs.

Neither child nor parents will have the same kind of access to one another after the marriage that they had before. Marriage is a developmental milestone for both of them. The marriage will change the way in which both relate to one another. Marriage has been called a passage into adulthood. Both parents and children will be experiencing a form of loss at this time although parents probably feel it more. Robert Stahmann and William Hiebert describe the difficulty in this way:

> Some families enable their children to go away, to become independent, and to be responsible, functioning adults. Other families hang on, making decisions for their children, interrupting the children's decision-making process, and continuing to take responsibility for them. In the process, these families cripple the ability of children to become independent and responsible. Thus, children enter late adolescence or young adulthood physically ready and able to enter marriage but still not adult in terms of their own responsibility and decision-making ability. These families have made so many decisions for their children that even as young adults, these children still need somebody to help them live, to get them up in the morning, to see to it that they go to work, and so on. It is as if these families somehow do not successfully resolve the young persons' dependency needs.[*][2]

*Reprinted by permission of the publisher, from Premarital Counseling by Robert F. Stahmann and William J. Hiebert (Lexington, Mass.: Lexington Books, D.C. Heath and Company, Copyright 1980, D.C. Heath and Company).

To initiate the discussion about in-laws and their influence upon the couple's life I ask, "How and where do you want to spend your first Thanksgiving and Christmas?" In practically all cases, the asking of this question elicits a strong response that usually is already an in-law conflict. Often parents assume that the new couple will fit into their own family traditions without allowing the couple any voice of their own.

One couple responded by saying, "We have already worked through that problem. Her folks and mine had already made plans for us. We told them however that we wanted our first Thanksgiving and Christmas to be special, and so we had rented a cabin in the mountains for the two of us. The parents aren't the happiest about the decision but they are accepting it. The next year then we can all work it out together where we will be."

There are several other questions to be asked. They include, How do you anticipate dealing with your parents after marriage? How do you anticipate dealing with your in-laws? How much time do you feel you will want to spend with your parents and in-laws in the first year of your marriage? How near do you plan to live to your parents or in-laws? If you visit one set of parents one week, do you feel that you need to visit the other set of parents that week? These are basic questions, but they are subject areas that have not been dealt with by most couples.

The information you receive back from the parents on their forms will help you in your discussion with the couple.

Why is it so important that individuals leave home psychologically? There are several important reasons. Those who have not left home keep getting caught up in family problems. Because of the crisis going on in the larger families their own marriage tends to stay in crisis. A second factor is that individuals who have not left home psychologically tend to look for partners who might continue the parenting that they received at home. They look for a person who will take care of them rather then being an equal partner. Those who have not yet separated from their parents usually come from homes in which the parents do not want them to separate.

In-laws can be an excellent resource in terms of emotional support and advice. Young couples need to look at them as they would at other friends. Looking at them with a positive attitude builds the relationship. If you are counseling a couple in which one individual is having difficulty with the other's parents, you could ask, "What might you have been doing to bring on this problem? What might they have been doing? What have you done to try to bring about a reconciliation?"

One time a young man in counseling said he felt that his fiancée's parents did not really like or even respect him. My initial response was, "How much time have you taken to sit down with them and allow them the privilege of getting to know you? Have you really shared with them some of the things of your life? Have you ever taken them out to dinner—and paid the bill?" He had done none of those things, so we developed a plan: during the next week he would spend time with them, talking about things that would be of interest to them, talking with his fiancée's father about his job, and getting to know them more. On Sunday the young couple took the parents to church and then to dinner. The results were very positive. The young man came back the next week and said, "You know, I never realized how much they cared for me." The main reason for the problem was that he was not reaching out. In order to have others respond to us, we cannot wait for them to take the initiative but must reach out ourselves.

There are certain guidelines about in-laws which can be shared with the couple. Some of these are just common sense principles. A person should treat his in-laws with the same consideration and respect that he gives to friends who are not in-laws. When in-laws take an interest in your life and give advice, do what you would do if a friend gave advice. If it is good, follow it; if it is not good, accept it graciously and then ignore it. Remember that many times when in-laws appear too concerned with your affairs, they are not trying to interfere in your life but are sincerely interested in your welfare. Look for the good points in your in-laws. When you visit them, make the visits short. When visiting the in-laws, be as thoughtful, courteous, and helpful as you are when you are at other friends'. Accept the in-laws as they are. Remember that they would probably like to make changes in you, too. Mothers-in-law have been close to their children before marriage; give them time to find new interests in life. Go into marriage with a positive attitude toward your in-laws. You believe it is a good family to marry into, and you intend to enjoy your new family. Give advice to your in-laws only if they ask for it. Express the faults of your spouse only to your spouse, not to your family. Do not quote your family or hold them up as models to your spouse. Remember it takes at least two people to create an in-law problem; no one person is ever solely to blame. (You may want to recommend the book *How to Be a Better-Than-Average In-law* by Norman Wright, Victor Books, 1981.)

You may want to have the preceding principles duplicated and available to give to the couple so they can take them home and restudy them. As you read this material to them, it is interesting to observe their reactions as the various points are covered. Now and then one might jab the other or look at the other with raised eyebrows, as they may have encountered problems already.

Communication is a critical topic for any couple. A question to ask is, "How do you communicate now, and what would you like to change about your communication style?" If a couple is having difficulty with their communication (and this is usually detected on the "Taylor-Johnson Temperament Analysis") I might ask them to take the "Premarital Communications Inventory," as it can indicate specific areas that we need to strengthen.

Sometimes I ask a couple to discuss a subject that they have not talked about much, or a controversial subject. It is healthy for the couple to disagree in your presence; it allows you to see some of the communication principles they might be employing to handle their disagreements. If they have such a discussion, ask them to sit face-to-face, to move their chairs so they are looking at one another. Many times married couples learn to communicate "from the hip," as we call it. They run past each other on the way to the other room, or the wife is in one room fixing the dinner, and the husband is in the other room reading the paper. They talk to one another but rarely have eye contact. I want the couple to experience looking into each other's face and to note some of the nonverbal communication. Once they are settled face-to-face, I sit back and let them talk for two or three minutes, or even for ten minutes.

Another method that will aid communication is to record the conversation (asking their permission to do so, and keeping the tape recorder out of their view). Then play back some of the discussion so that all of you can analyze communication. This can be a very enjoyable experience. People are surprised to hear how they express themselves to others.

As counselors we look at a couple to determine if they have the ability to share on a deep emotional and feeling level. We want them to be able to share their convictions, their ideas, their philosophies, and not only that, but how they feel about some of their ideas and beliefs. Many people communicate only on what we call the "cliché level." They talk about the weather; they talk about how they feel physically; they talk about some mundane subject, but they do not get down to serious problems and topics. They do not talk about their relationship. In premarital counseling, in a sense, we are forcing people to talk about items that they have not wanted to talk about but really need to discuss.

Counseling gives us an opportunity to share some basic principles of communication with the couple. A basis for communication is an atmosphere in which people can share their ideas and their beliefs, no matter what they are. We also emphasize that they cannot really avoid controversy, so they might as well learn to face some of the difficulties. Using the silent treatment against another person is very unfair and does not solve the problem. If you have a couple who already has this tendency, you could work with the more verbal individual and ask, When your partner retreats and becomes silent and won't communicate with you, how are you going to get him or her to communicate?

Often people who are verbal fall into the trap of putting pressure on that nonverbal person. They will say, "Why don't you talk to me? I want to listen to you. Tell me what you're thinking." And the more pressure they put on, the more the other individual withdraws. And the more the other individual withdraws, the more irritated and agitated the verbal one becomes and the more pressure he or she exerts.

One of the best ways to solve this problem is for the verbal person to say, "I do want to hear what you have to say, and I do want to listen. I'm also willing to wait until you find it comfortable to express yourself." Then back off and do not mention it again. It might take ten minutes; it might take an hour for the person to share. And when he does talk, it is imperative for the verbal one not to make value judgments such as, "Well, where did you ever get a ridiculous idea like that? That's really stupid!" If this happens the quiet one realizes that it is not worthwhile to share what he believes, because he will be criticized.

By now the couple may be reading the book on communication. If not, ask them to begin. After they have completed the first five chapters, have them bring in a list of the ten most important principles that will assist them in their life together.

During the next week or so they will be completing the chapters on communication and conflict resolution in *Before You Say I Do* that will assist the couple in further growth in this area. You might want to ask the couple during the fourth session if they have any questions or reactions to the chapter on need fulfillment in marriage.

From time to time you may find yourself in a situation where a couple is not using *Before You Say I Do* or you believe some of the projects should be done in your presence. If the topic area of need fulfillment is handled in the session, it is done in the following way.

Each couple is asked to take four sheets of 8½-by-11 inch paper and draw a line down the middle of each one. One sheet should be titled "Social Needs." Another should be called "Physical Needs," another "Emotional Needs," and the last, "Spiritual Needs." On the left-hand side of the page the individual should list as many of the needs as he or she can for this area of his life. On the right-hand side of the paper he/she should list what his future spouse could do to meet those needs. The couple does not talk about the lists during the week. They bring the lists with them to their session. Then each page is folded in half so that the list of needs is seen but the way the future spouse can fulfill those needs is folded under (the person reading the paper cannot read that portion). All four folded papers are exchanged with each other. Then each one (at home during the week) should read over the future spouse's list of needs and on a separate piece of paper write down what he thinks he can do to fulfill those needs. When the project is completed on all four areas of needs, the couple can then come together, open up the other side of their papers, and compare their ideas of how to meet the needs with the other's list. Then they can discuss this together.

Here is an example of what one woman wrote:

Emotional

My Needs	How Ken Can Meet Them
To feel loved, cherished	Call me, prepare me for sex, hold me, kiss me, look at me with glimmer in his eye, take naps so he will feel refreshed to be with me.
To feel supported, believed in	Pray for me in front of me and secretly as well. Challenge me, praise me, see my potential in specific situations.
To feel comforted when down	Hold me, let me cry on his shoulder, feel my hurt with me, be gentle and sensitive to my moods, let me know he notices them.
To feel not alone	Share my daily life's joys and sorrows, enter into the conversation about my day, be interested in daily details that help him understand me.
To feel respected and to respect	Continue saying please and thanks at meals. Replace things he uses up or takes out, clean up after himself, prepare himself to be with me mentally.

By now you have covered much of the content of the third and fourth sessions. There are occasions in which you will not cover it all in two sessions and may have to continue it into the fifth session.

Between the third and fourth sessions the couple is given several assignments that are due by the fifth session. First, they are asked to have Bible study and prayer together. Many couples have already started, but some have not. In fact, some have said, "What do we do? We've never done it before." This is an opportunity to share some basic principles with them. *Two Become One* by J. Allen Peterson is an excellent biblical study workbook covering some of the main areas of marriage. The couple can work on this together, and it gives them a structure that many are lacking.

They are also asked to list Scripture verses they feel they would like to build their marriage relationship upon. They are to do this by themselves without discussing it and to bring this to the fifth session. I ask them not to list passages such as Proverbs 31, Ephesians 5, or 1 Peter 3. Those passages are very important to the marriage relationship, but I ask the couple not to use them and to do some creative thinking about the rest of Scripture.

The final assignment is to write out in as much detail as possible the budget that they feel they are going to be able to live with when they are married.

I like to close the third or fourth session with a quote for them to consider, one that causes them to think and discuss. This is from Dr. Dwight H. Small's *Christian: Celebrate Your Sexuality*.

> When a man and a woman unite in marriage, humanity experiences a restoration to wholeness. The glory of the man is the acknowledgement that woman was created for him; the glory of the woman is the acknowledgement that man is incomplete without her. The humility of the woman is the acknowledgement that she was made for him; the humility of the man is the acknowledgement that he is incomplete without her. Both share an equal dignity, honor and worth. Yes, and each shares a humility before the other also. Each is necessarily the completion of the other, each is necessarily dependent upon the other.[3]

SUGGESTED OUTLINE FOR SESSIONS THREE AND FOUR

Test Results

1. Examine the T-JTA profiles and note the differences and the similarities between the individuals.
2. Ask them in what way their parents are like them. How is the couple like their parents? Which of the traits and qualities of their parents are the man and the woman looking for in each other?
3. Discuss results of the "Marriage Prediction Schedule."

Discussion of Homework Assignment

1. Ask what each is bringing to this marriage that will make it work.

2. Have them detail what each one's role and responsibility will be.
3. Ask what they would get out of marriage that they won't get if they remained single.
4. Discuss "Your Role Concepts Comparison Sheet" (found in the Appendix of this book).
5. Have each name the personal characteristics that he possesses that will build up a marriage. Have each name the personal characteristics his partner possesses that might tend to tear down the marriage.
6. Ask how each intends to change his mate.
7. Ask what they think of the material they're reading. (Remember to complete reading materials before the conclusion of the counseling sessions.)

Sex, the Honeymoon, and Children

1. Discuss the sexual relationship.
2. Discuss the need for a limited physical relationship before marriage.
3. Talk about the honeymoon and offer suggestions as given in this chapter.
4. Explore the couple's attitude toward children—how many they want to have and when.

In-laws and Parents

1. Ask what their attitudes are toward both sets of parents.
2. How close will the couple live to them? Does each feel that it would be possible for him to live a thousand miles away from his own parents?
3. How does each one anticipate dealing with parents after marriage?
4. How does each one anticipate dealing with in-laws?
5. How much time do they feel they will want to spend with parents and in-laws in the first year of marriage?
6. How near do they plan to live to parents or in-laws?
7. If they visit one set of parents one week, do they feel the need to visit the other set of parents that week?
8. Discuss the positive influence of in-laws.

Communication

1. How do they communicate now, and what would they like to change about communication style?

Assign Homework

1. Bible study and prayer.
2. List Scripture upon which to build a marriage.
3. Listen to one of the tapes on roles and responsibilities.
4. Prepare in detail a comfortable budget.

Close with quote by Small.

NOTES

1. Wes Roberts and Norman Wright, *Before You Say I Do* (Irvine, Cal.: Harvest, 1978), p. 24.
2. Robert F. Stahmann and William J. Hiebert, *Premarital Counseling* (Lexington, Mass.: Lexington Books, 1980), p. 19.
3. Dwight H. Small, *Christian: Celebrate Your Sexuality* (Old Tappan, N.J.: Revell, 1974), p. 144.

7

The Fifth Session

By now you may have discovered that there is so much material to cover that you question whether it can be done in the suggested number of sessions. But the fifth session gives you a chance to catch up on anything you have not covered so far. It is best to talk in detail about each topic so the couple reaches a solid understanding. In addition, they need to ask questions so they can apply this material to their lives.

Many questions have already been suggested for you to ask, but there are several more that you could cover with the couple. These deal with various subjects, and you can work them in where you see fit.

The first is, Do you like sympathy and attention when you are ill? That might sound like a strange question, but people come from different backgrounds. They have had different experiences; where one individual might like a lot of attention, the other might prefer to be left alone. If this is not discussed ahead of time, conflicts can arise. A wife, trying to care for her husband who has the flu, might give a tremendous amount of attention. But this irritates him. He does not appreciate it. She wants to know, "Why is he like this? I'm just trying to show him my love and compassion and concern." He does not see it in that way; or, for some reason, because of background experiences, he reacts negatively to it.

A second question is, As a general rule, do you enjoy the companionship of the opposite sex as much as that of your own sex? In this particular question we are trying to see how the people relate to both sexes. Here is a young woman who enjoys spending more time with men, perhaps because she is employed in a situation with more men than women. How is her husband going to react? Is this a trusting relationship? Is there any jealousy?

You can also ask, "After you're married, do you think that either of you will look at members of the opposite sex? Do you feel that in any way you might be attracted to members of the opposite sex?" Many different answers have come. Some say, "No, oh no, we're just completely suited for one another. We'll have no interest in another individual, and that's it." Others have been quite honest and stated, "Even during our engagement we've found that there are people who come into our lives that we might admire; and in some cases we might even be attracted to them." I have talked to a number of couples who have been surprised, shocked, disappointed, and even upset because, even on their honeymoon, they've discovered they notice members of the opposite sex, and are attracted to them. Honesty and realism are needed in this area.

Going into the marriage relationship with the idea that "we are never going to notice a person of the opposite sex" is unrealistic. Every man and woman will have to battle sexual temptation, particularly with the emphasis upon sex in our society, including the way people dress. We do try to clarify with the couple the fact that they will notice others and sometimes be attracted to them.

Many couples who have been married for some time have developed healthy relationships and can actually talk about others whom they admire or find very attractive. Some couples will talk about this quite openly. Often a husband will share with his wife that he is having trouble in his thought life at work because of the behavior and dress of the women. They talk about this very openly and his wife is not threatened in any way. They discuss it, they pray about it, and they work on it together. They do not hide these things from one another.

I like to suggest that if their relationship is what it should be, and their sexual relationship and love for one another are on a high plane, the couple is going to have less difficulty with temptation. This does not mean they will not notice and admire others. That is just part of being human, and physical beauty is part of God's creation. We can, however, caution them about what they do with their thought life. It is one thing to look at a person of the opposite sex and notice that he or she is attractive. But when one indulges in sexual fantasies concerning that individual, he is guilty of lust, which is sin. It is healthy for the counselor to share honestly. You could talk about this area and tell some of the ways you have learned to deal with it.

In concluding this area of discussion you may want to share with the couple this prayer from the book *Thank God for Sex* by Harry Hollis, Jr. The profound insights of this prayer have a lasting effect upon the couple.

Lord, it's hard to know what sex really is—
Is it some demon put here to torment me?
Or some delicious seducer from reality?
It is neither of these, Lord.

I know what sex is—
It is body and spirit,
It is passion and tenderness,
It is strong embrace and gentle hand-holding,
It is open nakedness and hidden mystery,
It is joyful tears on honeymoon faces, and
It is tears on wrinkled faces at a golden
        wedding anniversary.

Sex is a quiet look across the room,
    a love note on a pillow,
    a rose laid on a breakfast plate,
    laughter in the night.

Sex is life—not all of life—
but wrapped up in the meaning of life.

Sex is your good gift, O God,
    To enrich life,
    To continue the race,
    To communicate,
    To show me who I am,
    To reveal my mate,
    To cleanse through "one flesh."

Lord, some people say
    sex and religion don't mix;

But your Word says sex is good.
Help me to keep it good in my life.
Help me to be open about sex
    And still protect its mystery.
Help me to see that sex
    Is neither demon nor deity.
Help me not to climb into a fantasy world
    Of imaginary sexual partners;
Keep me in the real world
    To love the people you have created.

Teach me that my soul does not have to frown at sex
    for me to be a Christian.
It's hard for many people to say, "Thank God for sex!"
Because for them sex is more a problem than a gift.
They need to know that sex and gospel
Can be linked together again.
They need to hear the good news about sex.
Show me how I can help them.

Thank you, Lord, for making me a sexual being.
Thank you for showing me how to treat others
    with trust and love.
Thank you for letting me talk to you about sex.
Thank you that I feel free to say:
    "Thank God for sex!"[1]

A third question is, How much praise do you feel you need? Some individuals say they can exist with very little praise. However, they might need more than they realize, and it is crucial to determine how important praise is to each one.

We also talk about the area of friendship. You can ask, Do you like the friends of the person you're going to marry? Do you have many friends? How close are you to them? After you marry, how will you choose friends? Are you going to do this as a couple, or are you going to have your individual friends and go your separate ways? Often this contributes to conflict, because a young woman might not care for the friends of her future husband or the man dislikes friends of his future wife. Inwardly she would like him to give them up, but has not, as yet, verbalized this. Here it is brought out, talked about, and determined what can be worked out.

Another question is, What activities will you want to continue to do separately once you are married? One couple says, "We're

going to do everything together; nothing is going to be separate."
My response to them may be, "Is this realistic? Have you really
discussed this? Have you looked into it?" I ask both of them to tell
me about their hobbies and the things they enjoy. Then I ask, "Do
you see yourself doing this with your wife? Do you see yourself
doing this with your husband?" They may come to realize that
they have balance in their relationship already. Of course there are
many things a couple should enjoy doing together, but there may
be activities that one enjoys by himself.

Initially when a couple marries they may feel they need to
spend all their time together. This is why, when you talk to them
about the honeymoon, you could bring out some principles to
assist them, such as, When you go on your honeymoon, make sure
there are a number of activities. If you go to a place and just sit
there in a motel room for the next week or two, there is bound to
be some boredom; then some feelings may come out that are not
the healthiest for the marriage relationship. It is important that a
couple have activities together but also learn to do some things
separately.

I also like to pick up any questions or topics that we have not
covered previously, then talk about their proposed budget. How
realistic are they in terms of what it takes to live today? That is
what to look for. Often a couple has thoroughly worked this
through; other times there is a tremendous amount of unrealism. I
remember one couple who had gone into detail on the budget.
Both of them were working, and they went through every item and
had $350 to put into the bank each month. Together we worked on
that budget to determine the level of realism. Yet they still came
out with $250 they could put away. This couple had planned to
use both paychecks, but the future needed to be explored. I asked,
"What will happen if the wife becomes pregnant and you have to
rely upon one paycheck? Are you going to be able to do this?" If
both are working, it may be well to recommend that they try to live
on one paycheck so they become accustomed to that life-style.

Most couples I have worked with over the past few years have
not thought very much about what it takes to live. They might
come in and tell me that they have put aside $200 for their rent. I
may respond with "Fine. Where are you going to find a place for
$200? Have you looked?" They usually say, "No, we haven't really

looked, but we think we'll be able to find one." The next assignment is to send them out and ask them to look in the area where they want to live and see what they can find for $200. Perhaps they can find something, but they might not want to live in it.

We do the same with some of the other budget items. One couple, just recently, said that they could live on fifteen dollars a week for food. Neither had ever done any shopping. They both lived at home, and the parents were buying the food. It was a delightful experience to have them go to a market and see what they could buy for fifteen dollars. They quickly revised their budget. It is standard practice now to ask couples to shop at a market together and purchase a week's supply of food for their family. It might also be helpful if the man would accompany the woman as she shops in a department store to become aware of costs.

We go into great detail with the budget since so much marital disruption is caused by financial strain. Sometimes a couple leaves out insurance costs or clothing. One young woman said that she had set aside $20 a month for clothing. That is not realistic. Medical expense is another thing to keep in mind. Hospitalization insurance is an important factor. The tithe to the church is important; if a couple has not made any provisions for this, it should be discussed. This item ought to be on the top of the list.

A sample form, "Your First-Year Budget," is found in the Appendix of this book. This could be used in helping a couple determine their budget.

Several resources can be used to assist the couple with developing their financial skills. During this session, I use a form called the "Finances Questionnaire." (This is found in the Appendix and may be duplicated for use in premarital counseling.) Each person is given a copy and asked to answer each question quickly. After completing it, they are asked to exchange papers and note how their partner answered the questions. This may cause one or both some surprise, yet it helps them understand each other's priorities. They could be encouraged to continue their discussion of this inventory after the counseling session.

Several excellent money management and budget outlines and resources are available. Several of the best are suggested here, one of which should be mandatory reading. You may want to obtain all of them and then determine which would best suit your ministry. These resources could easily be used in a financial seminar for the congregation. *Christian Family Money Management and Financial Planning* is a twenty-four-page booklet which assists a couple in determining their assets as well as assisting them in planning a budget. This booklet and other helpful pamphlets are available from Louis Neebaver Co., Old York Road & Township Line, Benson East, Jenkintown, Pennsylvania 19046. *Handbook for Financial Faithfulness, a Scriptural Approach to Financial Planning*, by Floyd Sharp and Al MacDonald, is published by Zondervan.

Household Finance Corporation has developed an economical "Money Management Library" consisting of several forty- to fifty-page pamphlets on various helpful topics. This material may be included in the mandatory reading by the couple. The titles are *Your Health and Recreation Dollar, Your Shopping Dollar, Your Equipment Dollar, Your Home Furnishings Dollar, Your Housing Dollar, Your Clothing Dollar, Your Food Dollar, Children's Spending, It's Your Credit—Manage It Wisely,* and *Reaching Your Financial Goals.*

Other areas that need to be considered include the ways the two people have handled money in the past. Have they had a sufficient amount of money to handle? Have they had a savings account? Have they ever had a checking account?

Another question to consider is, When they are married, who is going to be responsible for handling the finances? Who will pay the bills and handle the checks? And how have they arrived at this particular decision? There seems to be discussion and controversy today over the idea that this must be the husband's responsibility. Now and then you find a man who says, "Well, I don't have a head for figures. I really haven't had any experience here." Whether it is the man or the woman who has not had financial experience both ought to develop financial proficiency. No matter who is paying the bills, both need to be fully aware of the amount of money coming in and where it is going. If a wife is responsible for purchasing groceries each week and the husband expresses concern over the amount of money she is spending, he should go shopping with her. That way he will know what it is like to go out and pay for food; he can see for himself what food costs.

Three basic principles to develop financial unity are: (1) All money brought in should be regarded as "family" money with each person informed of its sources and destination; (2) money should be used after mutual discussion and agreement; and (3) each person should receive a small amount for their own use without having to account for it.

Another principle to follow is to consider what the money will be spent for and then classify each item as a need or a want. Too often what we may consider needs are actually wants and thus are not essential. A resource that would be extremely beneficial to both the minister doing the counseling and to the couple is a series of tapes by Larry Burkett, "Christian Financial Management," that is available from Christian Marriage Enrichment. They should be loaned to the couple at this time.

A prior assignment was listening to the tapes on roles and responsibilities. Time is spent talking about their feelings about and reactions to the tapes, and whether they agreed or disagreed with them. Now and then someone will say, "I really can't believe everything that that man said on the tape." That's all right. Talk about it and see in what way he or she disagreed with it. Quite often they just say, "It was tremendous. I wish I'd heard teaching like that years ago." Different reactions are given, but the discussion helps clarify points on the tape.

Another prior assignment to discuss is the couple's time of Bible study and prayer together. How did they feel as they went through it? What did they experience? Some couples say, "Oh, it was very awkward at first. I'd never prayed in the presence of my fiancé before. But, you know, even though it was awkward, I really did enjoy it and it was a good experience. And when it came to Bible study, we just followed the outline that was given in that book *Two Become One*, and we filled in the questions and answers and then we talked about them and how they will apply to our marriage."

It is a valuable experience during the premarital counseling (and perhaps even earlier than I suggested) that a couple learn to pray together, to develop a time of sharing in the Word together, to discuss and talk about spiritual things. Often couples do feel awkward if they have not done it before. If they wait until after the marriage, they might not get into it. It's interesting to talk to some couples who say, "You know, it took us four years to pray together, because both of us were sitting back and waiting for the other one to suggest it. We didn't want to bring it up ourselves, so we just assumed the other person would." You, as the pastor-counselor, can be very helpful at this time; it would be well to share some of your own experiences while at the same time allowing the couple to develop the type of relationship that would suit them.

A helpful devotional book that the couple can read together is *Forty Ways to Say I Love You* by James R. Bjorge (Minneapolis: Augsburg, 1979).

For the rest of the session, consider the verses that the couple has selected to build their marriage relationship upon. They were asked to do this individually. We may start out with the young woman and ask her to share the verses and tell why she thinks these are important. This is the first time that her fiancé has heard these. After the woman has shared, the same process is repeated with the man.

Over the years I have gained a great deal from the insight, perception, and honesty of young couples as they have pointed out concepts that have been new to me or that I had never thought of before. We need to have a receptive attitude as we practice premarital counseling.

Next I spend ten to thirty minutes sharing the verses I want them to consider. The verses I use are printed in the Appendix under the title, "The Family Communications Guideline." I have these printed on good paper, and I give a copy to the couple. They have one in front of them and I have one in front of me. Some of these are a review and reinforcement of verses from their assigned reading. Many of the verses that I feel are important in building a marriage relationship have to do with communication.

After talking about communication, I read the letters their parents wrote. Most couples are very eager to hear these and to have a copy. Here are examples of two recent letters:

> We have prayed since Chuck was a young boy that the Lord would direct him in selecting his life partner. We are very pleased and excited that the Lord has led Chuck to Pattie. They met at Biola

and have had the privileges of getting to know each other these past two years. We are pleased that Pattie first of all loves the Lord and wants to serve Him and secondly loves Chuck and wants to be his mate and serve him.

Pattie has many fine qualities such as a very pleasing personality and is very loving and kind to others. She is concerned with others and above all wants to serve the Lord.

We feel that Pattie will fit into our family as if she always belonged. Chuck's two brothers love her as do his sister and grandparents. We consider her as another daugther. We are looking forward to many happy times together in the Lord and as a family. Our prayers will be continually with them.

Why We Appreciate Charles Becoming
Our Son-in-Law

There are many reasons why we appreciate Chuck, to become our son-in-law in less than two months. Here are just a few:

He is a fine Christian, raised in a wonderful, godly family—his parents, two brothers and sister have also shown their warmth and love—a great Church—Church of the Open Door, L.A.—and in training at Biola College.

His goals, aspirations and plans for Christian service are solid, as he plans to go on for further studies in Seminary . . .

He has so many of the character qualities described in Advanced Basic Youth Conflicts' Seminar and so complements Pattie well. He has helped to give her stability, purpose and new avenues of services, as he has drawn her out, with his outgoing personality.

He appears to be a man of prayer and devotion to God, with a desire to serve Him, as both Chuck and Pattie have set goals for His glory, for themselves—meaningful goals in Christian life and service for their future. This pleases us very much.

Chuck is very honest, direct, disciplined, organized (as seen in his school life and whole pattern of living), humble (seen in his sports, especially) and virtuous. He has high moral standards.

We have witnessed, over the past two years, especially in the last eleven months, sufficiently, to be convinced that he will take good care of Pattie, will provide for her and endeavor to make her life as much as God intends for it to be to the best of his ability. We believe he will strive for the highest and best for both of them, for God's glory.

His warmhearted generosity, sympathetic nature, keen interest in others and handsomeness are other additional features not to be overlooked.

We are thus very happy to have Chuck becoming the husband of Pattie. We pray daily for them both, asking God's will for them and their lives.

We could wish no greater joy than that they be full of Christ, His Holy Spirit and the Word, as they serve Him.

There are times when you will want to discuss significant comments from the parents' questions form, which they also filled out. The completed sheets should be given to the couple for they may want to discuss some of the responses with their parents.

Here is a sample of a list of expectations that a man's father wrote:

Eleven Expectations from Tom and Denise

1. Live their own life without outside interference from us.
2. To know we are available twenty-four hours a day for any reason whatsoever.
3. Expect that they will call us once a month if local and once every two months if out-of-state.
4. Expect them to live a good, healthy, normal life.
5. Expect them to abide by the Ten Commandments.
6. Expect them to propagate the population.
7. Expect that both will try to spread their religious beliefs and Bible findings in a constructive manner rather than by belittling or tearing down other religious beliefs.
8. Expect their love and devotion to one another to grow and their understanding of the rights and privileges of each other to expand.
9. Expect both Tom and Denise to maintain close relationships with their brothers and sisters. This I consider very important.
10. Financially, I expect Tom and Denise to make the best deal possible for themselves. I hope they'll never become wards of any group of society.
11. Expect they will keep themselves physically and mentally alert.

As a parent I have prayed and hoped that each of my children would find a lifetime partner—one who would be kind, understanding, and forgiving—one who would want children and rear them in a healthy Christian atmosphere—one who would cater to the wants and needs of the other—one who would place the raising of their children as their most important duty.

In Denise I find all the above traits and feel that her love for Tom will help carry him through the trials and tribulations of life, and am sure she will make my son happy. I, in turn, will be happy.

Stahmann and Hiebert, in their structure of premarital counseling, have a family-of-origin (FOE) exploration. It is conducted because the degree of separation a person has from his or her family of origin can effect marital success. In order to help the process occur they have a session entitled "Saying Good-bye." This concept as presented or with variations appears to have significant value.

We have added to the FOE an optional session which has to do with bringing both sets of parents into the last session with the premarital couple. If the counseling is being conducted by a nonclergy premarital counselor, this will be the last session. If it is being conducted by a member of the clergy, then the session with the parents can be the last session before part 4 (which deals with the wedding preparation) a part of the session on the wedding preparation; or the session following the one on the wedding preparation.

The premarital counselor does not have a contract to work with the parents on their marriages. He or she can, however, invite the parents to join in the last session. If the counselor wishes to include parents or step-parents in the final stage of the counseling process, we suggest that he or she should inform the couple of this intention at the beginning of the process. Not only is it important for the premarital couples to know, but it is also important for them to be coached by the premarital counselor in how to present the invitation to the parents. They can be instructed to indicate to the parents that marriage is a very special and meaningful event in the lives of people. As young people they are making a step like the one that their parents made many years ago. The counselor's invitation to the parents, then, helps them to connect with and celebrate this event in the lives of their children, which is also a reminder of the similar event that the parents celebrated.

We suggest that when the parents arrive for the session, the counselor begin by explaining why they were asked to come. In this explanation, the premarital counselor can talk about the theory of parental models. The point of this brief introduction is not to underscore any difficulty the children may have with leaving home, but rather to emphasize the concept that parents are indeed important models for children. The counselor explains that the bride and groom have observed sometimes without consciously knowing it their parents' marriages of eighteen, twenty, twenty-four, or however many years, and that these four people as objects of such observation, have been teaching their young people about marriage and family life.

As part of the explanation to parents, the counselor also can say, in the presence of all six, that he or she has discovered that most parents have had their own struggles with trying to carve out a successful marriage, in their early years especially. He or she can add that each marriage takes adjusting; some marriages take more adjusting than others.

Last, the counselor can indicate that the parents will no longer have the same kind of access to their children after the marriage that they had before. Here one can underscore the sense that marriage is a developmental milestone. Marriage changes the way in which people relate to each other. Not only does it change the way in which a man and woman relate to each other, but it also changes the way in which parents relate to adult children. Marriage is a kind of passage into adulthood, a milestone in the maturing process of human beings. While children are single, parents frequently feel they can offer the children plentiful advice. Once a child makes the move to marriage, that child is in effect saying to parents, "I am becoming an adult; I am going to do the very same things you do." While not all people experience marriage as the passage to adulthood, it is still valuable in helping the generations to separate for the premarital counselor to stress the importance of marriage as a developmental milestone.

All of this is a way of saying that with the marriage of their children, parents are experiencing a kind of loss. Children are also experiencing a kind of loss. Marriage marks a passage of time. The focus of the session with the parents, then, is an attempt to wrap up two basic elements: the changing nature of the parent-adult child relationship and the passing on of family wisdom (last advice).

We think it well for the premarital counselor to structure the session rather than turn it over to the family. Indicate to the parents that in this setting, they are being asked to give a last piece of wisdom to their children. Each will have his or her time to talk. This is their opportunity to say goodbye. The premarital counselor can aid the parents by asking or helping them to discuss two areas. First, what one piece of advice would they give their child about

Parent

how to succeed in marriage—advice they learned in their own marriage? Second, how are they going to continue their own marriage now that the child is moving on? How will their relationship now be different?

It is helpful for the premarital counselor to structure the rest of the session as well. Indicate which parents should go first; if one needs more time to think, pass on to the other. The premarital counselor has the responsibility of doing the talking.

When the parents have finished with what they have to say, the premarital counselor can summarize what the parents said as a way of recapping and heightening both the happiness and the poignancy of this session.

The session with the parents will probably be experienced as somewhat strange and tense but rewarding by the premarital counselor who has not had the opportunity to experience this process before. The more of these sessions that the premarital counselor conducts, the more efficient and successful they will be. It is important, however, to underscore our idea that if the premarital counselor is enjoying the task and having fun, the couple and the parents will too—and they will benefit from the process.*[2]

You will spend a lot of time discussing the details of the wedding ceremony with a couple. A pastor needs to be flexible because marriage ceremonies are changing today. Couples desire to write their own ceremonies, and they want to plan in greater detail than before. Many of them might choose to be married in a place other than the church sanctuary. They might prefer a home, a hillside, or a park. I think we need to allow for the changes that are coming about. Some of the wedding ceremonies young people have designed have been very creative and enriching, and they glorify the Lord. Many couples want more of a Christian emphasis, and a time of dedication and testimony in the service.

Here is an example of a creative approach to the wedding ceremony.

*Reprinted by permission of the publisher, from Premarital Counseling by Robert F. Stahmann and William J. Hiebert (Lexington, Mass.: Lexington Books, D.C. Heath and Company, Copyright 1980, D.C. Heath and Company).

Reaffirm Your Family Ties

Edwin R. Lincoln

The custom of giving the bride away has been criticized recently as archaic, inappropriate, and meaningless. Women are no longer chattels of the father and the husband. No longer does the father provide a dowry in terms of money, goods, or estate that his daughter brings to the marriage as compensation for the fact that she is a female (although some people suggest that the tradition of the bride's family bearing the brunt of the wedding expense is a persistent remnant of this earlier practice).

A father once said to me at a wedding rehearsal, "I'll go along with that part in the ceremony, but I really don't believe I'm doing anything significant by giving my daughter away. She was gone long before today!" In a sense that is true. The change in a parent-child relationship, which comes with maturity, starts long before a wedding day. The choice of a mate is only another symbol of what has been happening for years. Thus, in many churches, new and revised orders for the Service of Marriage either make the giving of the bride optional, or omit it altogether.

After twenty years of conducting marriage ceremonies, most couples I talk with still want their ceremony to include some acknowledgment of family ties. Some of them want something different from the traditional question, yet they agree that even though the original intention is no longer valid, the act still has significance.

The moment is packed with deep emotion. But you ought not solve a problem, nor meet a need, by just removing what is unsatisfactory. Replace it with something else. I suggest that we rename this portion of the marriage service and call it "Reaffirming Family Ties." I discuss this with every bride and groom. More and more couples respond positively. Here is the way it works.

The parents of the groom and the mother of the bride are led to their seats in the traditional manner. The father escorts the bride down the aisle. But when she gets to where the groom is waiting, her father immediately sits with his wife.

At the point in the ceremony where the bride is normally given in marriage, I ask both sets of parents to come forward and stand behind their son and daughter. This follows:

"Mr. and Mrs. _____; Mr. and Mrs. _____; I have asked you to come forward now because your presence at this time is a rich testimony of the importance of family ties. You have encouraged N_____ and N_____ to come to this moment in the spirit of creating a new family constellation. You are giving your children to life's adventure, and not merely away from yourselves.

"This is what you raise your children for; to let them go their way. And in their going, they come back again and again to share their discoveries and their joys with you. They confirm for you, who are parents, that you have fulfilled your task. Now, your new role is to support and encourage your son and daughter in theirs.

"It seems right, then, to ask you all, mothers and fathers, to make a vow, just as N_____ and N_____ will make theirs to each other in a moment.

"Do you support N_____ and N_____ in their choice of each other, and will you encourage them to build a home marked by openness, understanding, and mutual sharing?" (The parents will answer, "We do.") "Mr. and Mrs. _____ and Mr. and Mrs. _____; thank you for your good influence and steady ways that bring N_____ and N_____ to this day."

The parents may be seated at this point. However, I have seen some mothers and fathers pause a moment to exchange spontaneous signs of affection with the bride and groom through a brief embrace, a handshake, or a whispered word of love.

You might consider one final act in the ceremony to reinforce this reaffirmation of family ties. It is customary at the conclusion of the service to have the ushers return following the recessional and escort the mothers of the bride and groom out of the church, with the fathers walking behind. Why not have the parents leave with the wedding party, falling in step behind the last bridesmaid and usher? This visibly communicates that mothers and fathers, too, are an integral part of the ceremony, not just spectators. Also, from a practical standpoint, this eliminates that awkward pause between the time the ushers leave and return to get the mothers, who must leave before the guests can.

A word of caution. Some weddings do not have both sets of parents present. Through death or divorce, there may be only one parent on the bride's or groom's side. There are several other combinations possible. This situation does not mean you must reject the idea of reaffirming family ties. But it will require additional sensitivity to the feelings of the parents, some assurance that they are secure in their single status, and some slight revision in the service itself.

Not all couples or parents will want to try this. But enough of them will to confirm your decision to talk about it with them. The ones who choose to stay with the tradition will have had an opportunity to think about marriage as a rite of passage that not only floods a new home with joy, but also flows back into the homes from which the new husband and wife both came.[3]

Many books, both secular and Christian, are now available concerning the details of the wedding ceremony.

Here is a listing of some of the purposes for a wedding. You may want to think about these and incorporate some of them.

1. The partners' public affirmation of each other as spouses: The wedding is a public demonstration by the couple to their relatives and friends as well as to all society (in a sense, "to whom it may concern") of the couple's change in status.

2. The public affirmation of the partners' separation from their childhood homes: In anticipating a wedding, relatives and friends can express their feelings to the partners rather than keeping them hidden until after the wedding and then later berating the couple (now married) with statements such as, "I wish you had never married," or, "I knew it would not work out." By their attendance at the wedding, relatives and friends affirm their positive support of the couple and their intention to assist them in creating a good marriage.

One way in which this change of status is made explicit in some traditions is through the phrase "Who gives this woman to this man?" This may be interpreted only as a carry-over from earlier times when it was assumed that a woman must be "protected" at all times by the stronger (patriarchal, authoritarian) man—first her father, and then her husband. A modern psychological interpretation, however, is that the mother and father of each partner, the groom as well as the bride, openly admit that they no longer have first claim or first rights to their married child. Perhaps we should modify this part to allow also for the parents of the groom to give their adult son to his wife. Psychologically, unless such "giving" (or cutting of apron strings) occurs, then the stage is set for bad feelings of many types between the partners, parents, and in-laws.

3. A religious and philosophical affirmation: If the wedding is in a religious tradition, it includes the affirmation by the partners that God is a witness to their commitment to each other. In some

religious traditions, the wedding is considered to be a covenant between the partners and God.

4. A public examination of the voluntary commitment of each person to the other: The traditional phrase "Will you have this woman/man . . . " is a formal way of assuring that neither party is being forced into a marriage that she or he does not want. If someone opposes the marriage, the reasons should have been explored long before the wedding.

5. Evidence of the wedding commitment: The wedding provides for gifts that confirm the joining of two persons into the one unit of marriage. The wedding rings and other tokens that may be exchanged during the ceremony are visible symbols of the wedding pledge to each other. Handclasps, embraces, and other expressions may also demonstrate this covenant.

6. A legal confirmation: Although usually not mentioned during the wedding ceremony, the official (rabbi, priest, minister, or state-appointed official) who solemnizes the marriage must complete the marriage license and return it to the proper court for entry as a public record of the marriage.

7. A unique real life event: The wedding actually occurs in history at a given time and place. That may seem obvious, yet it means that later, in times of difficulty, there is no way for either party to deny the reality of the commitments that were made at the wedding. For many persons, their first wedding will be their only one. For those who may marry more than once, the experiences of the first wedding ceremony cannot be repeated.

8. A statement of the conditions of the marriage: In most ceremonies the bride and groom commit themselves to each other regardless of whatever difficulties may come ("better or worse, rich or poorer, sickness or health").

For those partners who want an unconditional commitment to each other, with no escape, the traditional phrase "until death us do part" makes this complete commitment very clear. In most traditions this phrase does not refer to a quantity of time (such as fifty years) but rather to the determination of a partner to continue to be committed to his or her spouse throughout any and all of the circumstances human living may bring. It is a way of saying, "My love and concern for you will continue, regardless of any circumstances that human living may bring."[4]

When you are coming to the end of the counseling with the couple, you might make some suggestions for their honeymoon. The honeymoon can be a time of spiritual growth and development. I suggest that they read through the book of Proverbs, finding every passage that would help to build their marriage relationship, specifically those passages dealing with one's emotional life and with communication. I also recommend that they get a copy of Paul Tournier's book *To Understand Each Other* (Atlanta: John Knox, 1967) and read this aloud to one another as a devotional guide. One other resource that I like to ask them to read out loud is the Song of Solomon (*Living Bible* version), because it's a very beautiful portrayal of love in the physical relationship.

Two books that I enjoy giving to couples as their wedding present are *The Living Marriage* by H. Norman Wright (Old Tappan, N.J.: Revell, 1975) in which is a compilation of Scriptures from the *Living Bible* along with helpful quotes from other sources. The other is *Into the High Country* by H. Norman Wright (Portland, Ore.: Multnomah, 1979). The couples have been very delighted with these for they have helped them and they have expressed their appreciation for these resources.

Before concluding premarital counseling, I remind the couple of their postmarital visit. There are important reasons for this visit; basically, it is to provide them with an opportunity to share how their relationship has been developing, and what they have learned and discovered. It also gives them an opportunity to bring up questions or problems. Some couples need two or three postmarital sessions to work out problems that have arisen. I tell them that it is their responsibility to call me. However, if I don't hear from them, then I will call and ask them to come in.

A last point to stress is that if they ever experience serious difficulties in their marriage relationship, they should never hesitate to seek help. Often pride, particularly on the part of the man, keeps them from seeking assistance. If they have tried to work out the problem and have not come to any solution, or if one is so frustrated that they just cannot see daylight, they ought to go to their pastor or to a professional counselor. One of the worst problems that can develop is a couple's waiting too long to go for professional help. In fact, many marriage counselors say that it takes approximately seven years from the onset of a problem before a couple seeks assistance. Such delay makes it very difficult for a counselor or pastor to be of much help.

If a married person is having difficulties, it is important that he or she communicate with the spouse first and be careful about talking over problems with friends. It is important that we have close friends, but we need to go to our spouse first. If we do seek out a friend, are we seeking him out for assistance, or for sympathy and to take our side? If a woman wants to talk over a problem with a friend, she ought to talk to another woman; a man ought to talk to another man. If one goes to an individual of the opposite sex, entanglements can develop.

For the last premarital visit, or the postmarital visit, some pastors have the couple over for dinner to spend time with the entire family. After a time of fellowship, the pastor and the couple can talk privately.

A time of prayer together usually concludes the premarital counseling sessions.

Now we need to discuss situations in which it would be difficult to perform the wedding ceremony. Even though this was discussed earlier, it is important to reinforce some of the principles. I believe that age is one of the factors that may lead a pastor to decide against the wedding. Several states now have laws prohibiting the marriage of individuals under a certain age. The state of California prohibits persons under the age of eighteen from being married unless they have parental consent and a court order giving permission. Some courts require premarital counseling before issuing an order.

You might encounter a couple who are both eighteen; even though they meet the legal requirements, you need to consider other factors. It is difficult, yet essential, to confront them with the facts about couples who marry at this age: they are more prone to divorce, they are losing out on friendships, perhaps they have not dated much, and many difficulties can arise. But, after counseling, you still might marry some of these couples because they are mature enough to make it work.

Tender age is not the only consideration. What happens if a man of thirty-five wants to marry a woman who is twenty-two? There is an age difference but they might be very close in maturity level, in emotional stability, and in their Christian walk. How would you feel about a couple if the woman is thirty-five and the man is twenty-two? An attitude in our society implies that it is all right for the man to be much older than the woman, but not the reverse. Our culture feels that such a marriage is not proper and that there are too many problems. Now and then you may run into such a couple, and you must examine your own attitudes. Such a couple might have a very good relationship.

What about some of the other problems that we encounter? When a couple refuses or fails to complete the assignments, it is an indication that their motivation level is so low that they will probably not work on problems that will arise in their marriage. In order for them to stay in the premarital counseling, they must complete the assignments. If they fail to complete their assignments, then I talk to them. I point out that this is an indication to me that their motivation level is too low for a marriage relationship. They must be willing to work on their marriage; they have to be willing to grow and move ahead in their life together. I might ask them to postpone the wedding until they see the importance of making an effort. If too many differences show up on the "Taylor-Johnson Temperament Analysis" test and the "Marriage Prediction Schedule," if they have a low ability to adjust, and if they are not concerned about changing, then I would not feel comfortable marrying them.

When you tell a couple you cannot marry them, you will find different reactions. It is helpful to formulate beforehand the words you will say and how you will say them, giving reasons and showing what you feel would be the probable consequences of their marriage at this time. Some couples might become hostile. They might say, "We can go down the street and find another church, and the pastor there will perform the ceremony. We don't have to be married here." Or somebody might say, "My father is a deacon in this church and he's going to be very unhappy with you, pastor." These are possibilities. You are going to have other couples who sit in stunned silence and say, "We really never thought of it that way before." Perhaps six months later this couple will come back and will be ready for marriage.

Some couples will be relieved upon hearing your decision. They have been waiting and hoping for someone to confront them and let them know that their marriage will not work out. It takes boldness and sensitivity on the counselor's part. We need to pray about this decision and think it through carefully, for we are influencing not just one life, but two—not only separately, but together in a marriage relationship.

<h2 style="text-align:center">Suggested Outline for Session Five</h2>

MARITAL ADJUSTMENT

1. Do they both like sympathy and attention when they are ill?
2. As a general rule, do both enjoy the companionship of the opposite sex as much as that of their own sex?
3. After they're married, do they think that either of them will look at members of the opposite sex? Do they feel they might be attracted to members of the opposite sex?
4. Share prayer from *Thank God for Sex* by Harry Hollis, Jr.
5. How much praise does each feel he needs?

FRIENDSHIP

1. Do they like their fiancé's friends? Do either have many friends? How close is each one to their friends? After they marry, how will they choose friends? Will they do this as a couple, or will they have individual friends and go separate ways?
2. What activities will they want to continue to do separately once they are married?
3. What hobbies and activities does each enjoy? Will they do any together?
4. Discuss the need for activities, especially on the honeymoon.

BUDGET

1. Discuss "Your First Year Budget," found in the Appendix of this book.
2. How have they handled money in the past? Has each had a sufficient amount of money to handle? Has each had a savings account?
3. Has either of them ever had a checking account?
4. When they are married, who will be responsible for handling the finances? Who will pay the bills and handle the checks? How have they arrived at this particular decision?

5. Share principles from this chapter on developing financial unity.

DISCUSSION OF HOMEWORK ASSIGNMENT

1. Discuss reactions to the tape on roles and responsibilities.
2. Discuss couple's time of Bible study and prayer together. How did they feel as they went through it? What did they experience?
3. Discuss prayer together.
4. Have the couple share the verses they found upon which they can build their marriage. Have them explain why they think these are important.
5. Pastor shares verses. See "The Family Communications Guideline" in the Appendix.
6. Share letters from the couple's parents.

WEDDING PLANS

1. Discuss ceremony details.
2. Make suggestions for honeymoon.

POSTMARITAL COUNSELING

1. Remind the couple of their postmarital visit.
2. Encourage them to seek help if needed.

CLOSE in prayer.

NOTES

1. Harry Hollis, Jr., *Thank God for Sex* (Nashville: Broadman, 1975), pp. 11-12. Used by permission.
2. Robert F. Stahmann and William J. Hiebert, *Premarital Counseling* (Lexington, Mass.: Lexington Books, 1980), pp. 79-80.
3. Edwin R. Lincoln, "Reaffirming Your Family Ties," cited in *Christianity Today*, 19 January 1979, pp. 32-33. Copyright 1981 by *Christianity Today*. Used by permission.
4. Richard Hunt and Edward Rydman, *Creative Marriage* (Boston: Holbrook Press, 1976), pp. 132-34.

8

Special Problems in Premarital Counseling

You will see couples who have unique situations. As much as possible, you need to plan your procedure and develop a standard to help you decide when a couple is ready for marriage. Your standard will be tested as you apply it to varying situations.

What happens if you have a widow or a widower in your church who wants to marry? Perhaps both partners have been married before, or perhaps one has been married and one has never been married. At this stage in life do they really need to go through premarital counseling? And yet, why not? If a man was married for thirty years, was widowed, lived alone for five years, and now plans to marry a woman who has never been married before, counseling is very necessary. Every newly married couple faces adjustments, and especially a couple such as this.

For example, you may encounter a couple where he is sixty-five and she's sixty-eight. She was married for forty years and he was married for thirty-five years. Now they have fallen in love and want to be married. Working with such a couple can be one of the most delightful experiences of your life, because they have so much to offer and share. But you as a pastor have a lot to offer them, too. They might be living in the past, holding on to the memories of those wonderful years, or maybe those not-so-wonderful years, with the other person; maybe they are going to bring these memories into the new marriage relationship. You have to look at their areas of expectations and adjustments and also their ability to adapt and adjust at this time.

No matter what their age or circumstances are, questions must be considered if children are a part of this newly formed family: Can the person who may never have been married before accept the experiences of the other's love life with someone else in years gone by? If there are children still in the home, can the new partner accept and love them? Will the children accept someone else in mother's or father's place? If one has never married before, can he or she suddenly take on a ready-made family and adjust to them? Often, the new parent fails to understand the psychological problem of the stepchild and may retaliate by rejecting the child, or by showing favoritism if his children are involved. When older children are involved they could oppose the marriage and even from the beginning of courtship manifest hostility toward the new partner.

If one has never been married, he or she must be able to accept the fact that the spouse has loved another, perhaps had children by the other, and that a big part of his or her life was inseparably involved with someone else and always will be. He or she must see that love objectively and accept it as a part of the new partner. To expect one never to talk about the first mate, never to look at the picture, is hardly reasonable. It is healthy to encourage the mate to talk about the first spouse, not to compare with the present one, but to help him to accept the present one in the other's place. It is very damaging for either to bring up the first relationship with such remarks as "John never treated me as you do," or "Mary never would have said that."

Another potential problem that arises now and then is, "What do you do with interracial marriages? What does the Bible have to say about this?" It does not appear that the Scripture has anything to say about interracial marriages. You are probably going to have more and more couples from different races wanting to be united in marriage. What will you say to a Christian couple who are of different nationalities and different backgrounds?

If I were counseling an interracial couple, I would want to know their motivations for marriage, as with any other couple. Are they mature individuals? Are they really in love, or is this marriage a reaction against parents or society? Are they trying to prove something? Have they really looked at some of the particular problems that will occur because of a marriage like this? It would be helpful to them to take the time to speak with other interracial couples who have been married for a number of years, couples who have had a successful experience, so that they go into marriage very realistically.

There are several main adjustment factors that a couple in a mixed marriage will face in varying degrees. The first is that of housing. In spite of legal action with civil rights boards, many mixed couples find resistance to their settling in various sections of cities and in many churches.

A second problem faced by the interracial couple is that of companionship with other families. Judson T. and Mary G. Landis said, "Young people who make mixed marriages while in a university community, where attitudes are likely to be more inclined toward acceptance of such marriages than in other communities, may encounter new problems if they leave the university community and settle elsewhere."[1] The couple may have to find more of their companionship with each other than the normal couple does. This, too, can add strains to a relationship which it may not be able to handle.

An interracial marriage will probably face in-law problems. Many families, including some who reared their children to be very liberal in racial attitudes, cannot accept the idea that their child is going to marry someone of a different race.

The greatest problem faced by this couple is the difficulty of rearing children who are marginal to two different cultures. The adjustments faced by the couple in an interracial marriage can be insignificant in comparison to those faced by children of such a marriage.

Dwight Small said:

> Not infrequently there is a very dark child and a very light one in the same family. The colored child loves the colored parent and dislikes the other. Or the parent takes to the child of the same color but rejects the other. This is aggravated when other children make fun of the fact that two children in the same family are different in color. Our cruel and competitive culture still brands such children as "half-breeds." So the crucial question is whether parents have

the right to impose upon unborn generations a radical decision of their own.[2]

Albert Gordon stated,

> Persons anticipating cross-marriages, however much in love they may be, have an important obligation to unborn children. It is not enough to say that such children will have to solve their own problems "when the time comes." Intermarriage frequently produces major psychological problems that are not readily solvable for the children of the intermarried. Living as we do in a world that emphasizes the importance of family and religious affiliations, it is not likely that the child will come through the maze of road blocks without doing some damage to himself.[3]

Children may be the recipients of cruel remarks and other unpleasantness. People can be hostile and cruel, and these factors must be considered.

Evidence indicates that couples contemplating an interracial marriage face many obstacles to adjustment and happiness. When a couple disregards the need for similarity of racial background, they could encounter adjustments that could be overwhelming.

There are many other individual cases that you will have. No matter what couple comes to us, we need to develop a standard, based as much as possible upon the Word of God, and we must hold to that standard. We have to educate the congregation concerning this policy. In time, our congregations will realize the importance of marriage and will appreciate our stand.

Here are two different cases. Consider some of the problems that they present, and decide how you would handle each one. What would you suggest, and what would you do?

The first case has to do with a young man, Richard, who is telling the story of his background. Think about what you would say to him if he were there in your study sharing this with you:

> My father divorced my mother when I was only two and a half. I guess I was her only real happiness after that. She never remarried, and I was the only child she ever had. Sometimes when I was little I wasn't sure if I really did make her happy. She cried a lot and it was very hard for me to distinguish whether she was crying because my father was gone or whether she was crying because she was happy I was there. She was always very sensitive. Things other

people said hurt her, and even when I was just growing up she'd come to me for comfort. It seemed to make her feel better to tell me her problems even though she knew that I, as a child, couldn't do anything about them.

She tried to do everything she could for me. She went without new clothes herself so that I could have everything I needed. She worked long hours, and part of the time she had a second job doing work at home. I used to feel terribly guilty about it, but she would always say, "There, there, you're my little boy to take care of now, but someday you will be my big man to take care of me." We were very close.

I started sleeping in her bed soon after my father left. I still do. I don't tell anybody that because they would think it was kind of queer for a grown man to be sleeping with his mother, but there's nothing sexual about it. I guess it's habit. I don't like to sleep alone any more than she does.

When I got to high school, I didn't have many dates. I was sort of shy and not very athletic. I didn't have much chance to play with the other boys. I'd been too busy with my studies because that's what Mother encouraged me to do. The girls didn't pay much attention to me either. I turned out to be kind of sensitive, too. My feelings were easily hurt. They still are.

My senior year in high school Mother started getting sick. I had talked some about going away to the state university, but when I found out the anxiety connected with my leaving made her even sicker, I decided not to do that and I went to college right here in town. She continued to have some types of illnesses and the doctors have never decided exactly what it is, but everything that upsets her now puts her to bed for a few days. While I was in college I went out with a few girls. I might have gone out more often but I couldn't stand to think of Mother sitting home alone.

When I got to graduate school, I met Ruth and for the first time I think I experienced some real feelings of love. It upset Mother terribly for me to talk about it. Mother didn't like her. She pointed out to me a lot of things that I probably should have seen myself about Ruth. She was from a different background and she was very selfish. Anyway, I broke up with her after about a year. That was eight years ago. My mother is much older now and I guess I'm her only source of support because economically, emotionally, she literally lives for me.

Recently I met a girl named Janice and I've been going with her about six months. Now Mother is starting to talk about her the same way she talked about Ruth, but worse. Janice says that I have to choose between her and my mother. I just can't do that. What am I going to do?

In many ways Richard is an emotional infant. He is very, very dependent upon his mother and he does have to come to the place where he makes a choice, but the choice is not all or nothing. He can learn to become more independent from his mother. She might try to manipulate him and she might threaten suicide. Her illness could become worse. Yet one of the healthiest events that could occur is for Richard to proceed to become more of a man and to develop his own life. She is trying to control him. Before he marries Janice, Richard will need counseling so that he can develop into the type of man that he should be. A pastor might even find occasion to talk to Richard and his mother or Richard and Janice or perhaps all three of them together.

Here is a different problem. Mary was a very attractive woman, a twenty-eight-year-old fashion designer. But she was extremely critical. She seemed to find something wrong with every man she went out with. She said,

I like to have a good time, but after I go out with a fellow for several weeks I just begin to see how many faults he has and just about that time he starts to get serious and wants to paw me. I've got a well-paying job and a beautiful car. My life is very convenient and well planned. Many times I've said to myself, "Why should I marry someone just for the sake of being married?"

The other girls try to make me feel as if I am missing something but I thought I knew better. I'm still sure I know more about love and more about men than most of them will ever learn. My mother was married twice, and both times it was to an irresponsible man who failed to provide for us. My father was the first one; he was an alcoholic. He had an overwhelming need for affection and response. He tried all the time to beg, demand or buy my love. Even as a tiny child I had to live with complex emotional problems. I had to learn to see through and sometimes give deceptive satisfactions to his impossible demands. I knew all about the weaknesses of men long before I started going out.

Unfortunately my father didn't stop when my mother divorced him. In fact, I think it got worse. He needed me more than ever. He used to call me long distance when I was in school. I didn't know what to say to him. I didn't know what to say to him then, and I don't know now. I just try to do the best I can, but that's never good enough.

After my father left, my mother married someone else just like him. It would almost be funny if it weren't so tragic. She used to swear that if she ever got out of the situation she was in, she'd never look at another man as long as she lived. But she wasn't unmarried a year before she found another man to abuse her. In many ways he was worse.

Now I'm twenty-eight. It hit me all of a sudden that in another ten years I'm going to be too old to have children, and I don't have much to live for right now. Last week for the first time in a long while a man was really serious about wanting to marry me. John's a nice guy; he's not very exciting though. But he's nice. I don't really love him, but I am fond of him, and I do know if I go ahead and marry him I'll start looking for his faults right from the wedding day. I just can't seem to help myself, and I know that I'll try to manipulate him, and I'm sure I can do it because I've had lots of practice. In some ways I guess I could be good for him because I think he really needs me. I know how to cheer him up and make him feel successful. My problem is, what should I do at this point? I don't know.

What are some of the basic problems that Mary has that are going to hinder a marriage relationship?

A person like this needs individual help before she will be ready for marriage. It could be that this young woman is very critical of herself. That could easily lead to the criticism of men. It is also a factor that her poor experiences with men and her ability to manipulate them have caused her to develop a bad attitude toward males in general. Before she considers marriage she should look into her own life and deal with some of her basic attitudes. She should probably not go through with this particular marriage. Fondness is one thing, but deep love is something else. A marriage relationship requires an ability to adjust and to accept oneself and another individual.

One other area that must be considered is a situation that occurs more and more today. Couples come in and say, "Why bother to be married? We're Christians, we've submitted ourselves to one another and we're living together. Isn't that marriage in the sight of God?"

One could take time debating whether a person is really

married or "not" married. The piece of paper and the ceremony do not necessarily make it more of a marriage, but we need to consider that one of the marks of a Christian is that his or her life should not be the cause of anyone's stumbling. The Christian's life is a witness to others, and it reflects the love of Jesus Christ. A relationship should avoid the very appearance of evil, according to the Scripture. In our society we have certain laws that we are expected to follow. A Christian couple that decides, "We don't need that piece of paper in order to be married," may cause others to stumble.

Dr. David Freeman, professor of philosophy at the University of Rhode Island, wrote an article titled, "Why Get Married?" It is published in the *Theology News and Notes* of Fuller Seminary. He was speaking to the question, Who needs a piece of paper in order to be married? and he said,

> To the Christian couple, the answer is simple: you do, not because it will insure that your love will mature more quickly, not because the license or the ceremony will insure the permanence of your love, but because the Christian is under obligation to obey laws that insure the wellbeing of their neighbor, laws including fairness and fulfillment of contractual obligations. Our society is complex. We are related to others by many crisscrossing, interlocking relationships. The relationship between two people in real love, while personal and intimate, is not solely private. It is a public affair. Two people shipwrecked on a desert island would hardly need a license or a minister to marry them. Their relationship would undoubtedly be private, with God alone as a witness. But the rest of us live in a community, belong to a family, are citizens of a state, and are dependent upon numerous individuals and organizations for our very survival. Marriage is a relationship between man and woman intended by God to be a monogamous relationship, intended to be a permanent bond in which many needs are satisfied—the need to love and be loved, the need for deep friendship, for sharing, for companionship, for sexual satisfaction, for children, the need to escape loneliness. Marriage ought to be a bond of love, reflecting the love Christ has for His people, a bond of sacrificial love where husband and wife have become one, one flesh, a unity.[4]

NOTES

1. Cleveland McDonald, *Creating a Successful Christian Marriage* (Grand Rapids: Baker, 1975), pp. 288-94, adapted.
2. Dwight H. Small, *Design for Christian Marriage* (Old Tappan, N.J.: Revell, 1959), p. 149.
3. Albert I. Gordon, *Intermarriage* (Boston: Beacon, 1964), p. 354.
4. Daniel Freeman, "Why Get Married?" *Theology News and Notes* 19, no. 4 (December 1973): 17.

9

Group Premarital Counseling and Preparation

This series on marriage preparation is designed to be used with a minimum of four couples and a maximum of fifteen. Premarital counseling usually involves one couple meeting for several sessions with the pastor or another staff member. This is the ideal. However, it is possible to combine individual premarital counseling of couples with group counseling. The couples can learn from one another during the group sessions. If several couples are planning to be married within a brief span of time, the group sessions can also save the pastor time.

In order to prepare yourself for this type of teaching situation, you may want to read *Ways to Help Them Learn—Adults* by H. Norman Wright, published by Regal. This book outlines, in detail, learning principles and teaching methods that will be used in this series.

Please be sure that you begin your own preparations in advance and carefully follow the advance preparation suggestions for materials to read, order, select, and reproduce.

Cost: Include $25-30 with the wedding service or church fee. This fee will cover the purchase of materials, tests, tapes, film rental, duplicating materials, and any other costs incurred. (The purchase of tapes is a one-time expense; they can be used again.) Part of the money should be used to purchase a set of the recommended books for each couple so they can keep these to read again. Some couples may ask if they can obtain copies of the tapes used in the series. The church could have an extra supply available or let the couples order them directly from the publishers.

Leaders for this series: The pastoral staff can be involved in conducting this series. It is also possible to train selected married couples to conduct the series. The training consists of having several married couples actually go through this course and having them listen to any tapes suggested.

Time: These sessions should be started at least three months before the wedding. The meetings could be conducted on any evening for two and three-quarters hours—from 7:00 to 9:45—including a fifteen-minute coffee break.

Schedule the meetings one week apart.

Advance Preparation Section
Prior to the sessions

I. For your own preparation:
   A. Be sure you have completed the first portion of this book.
   B. Be sure you read over this entire series before you set up the program.
II. Materials you will need for the series (order all materials at least one month in advance):
   A. Books: a copy of each of the following for each couple
      1. Coble, Betty. *Woman: Aware and Choosing.* Nashville: Broadman, 1975.
      2. Dobson, James. *What Wives Wish Their Husbands Knew About Women.* Wheaton, Ill.: Tyndale, 1975.
      3. Wheat, Ed, and Wheat, Gail. *Intended for Pleasure.* Old Tappan, N.J.: Revell, 1977.
      4. Wright, H. Norman. *Communication—Key to Your Marriage.* Glendale, Calif.: Gospel Light, Regal, 1974.
      5. Roberts, Wes, and Wright, Norman. *Before You Say I Do.* Irvine, Cal.: Harvest House, 1978. Each person will need a copy.
   B. Cassettes
      1. Wheat, Ed. "Sex Technique and Sex Problems in Marriage." Christian Marriage Enrichment, 8000 E. Girard, Suite 601, Denver, Colo. 80231.

2. Wright, H. Norman. "Communication—Key to Your Marriage." Christian Marriage Enrichment (see address above).

C. Tests
1. "Marriage Expectation Inventory for Engaged Couples." Saluda, S.C.: Family Life Publications.
2. "Sex Knowledge Inventory." Saluda, S.C.: Family Life Publications.
3. "Taylor-Johnson Temperament Analysis." Los Angeles: Psychological Publications.

D. Reserve the films *We Do! We Do!* and *Johnny Lingo* for the appropriate meetings. Order from a Christian film distributor or Augsburg Films, 3224 Beverly Blvd., Los Angeles, Calif. 90057.

E. Select speaker for the finances presentation and select three couples for the final meeting.

F. Prepare transparencies in advance and have an overhead projector and screen at each meeting.

G. Have paper and pencils available at all sessions.

STEP-BY-STEP PROCEDURE FOR EACH SESSION

Carefully read the instructions for each session. Prepare in advance any materials needed for the session. Check the instructions below and compare them with the session instructions so you will know that you have made all the necessary preparations.

SESSION	WHAT TO ORDER OR PREPARE PRIOR TO EACH SESSION
1.	1. Prepare transparencies.
	2. Be certain films are ordered. *We Do! We Do!* is used for session 1.
	3. Listen to the tape and select the section on the definition of marriage from the tape "Foundations of a Christian Marriage." (This tape is part of the series "Communication—Key to Your Marriage.") Have the tape set at this point so you can play the proper section at the right time.

4. Have the "Marriage Expectation Inventory for Engaged Couples" and the "Sex Knowledge Inventory" available.
5. Have available the book *Communication—Key to Your Marriage*.
6. Have a 16-mm projector and a cassette tape recorder available.
7. Duplicate copies of "Love Dies," found in the Appendix.
8. Have available copies of the form that the prospective in-laws complete. Duplicate four per couple.

2.
1. Have the T-JTA test booklets and answer sheets available.
2. Have available copies of *Intended for Pleasure* by the Wheats.
3. Prepare copies of "Case Studies on Conflicts in Marriage," found in the Appendix of this book.
4. Have the "Sex Knowledge Inventory" available.

3.
1. Have a set of Ed Wheat's cassettes available for each couple.
2. Have 3 × 5 cards available.
3. Prepare transparencies.
4. Have the film *Johnny Lingo* and a 16-mm projector available.
5. Obtain and read *Christian: Celebrate Your Sexuality* by Dwight H. Small (Revell).

4.
1. Prepare the "What Is Your Opinion" agree-disagree sheet.
2. Have the tape "Communication Is the Key" available.
3. Have the T-JTA profiles available.
4. Prepare transparencies.
5. Have books and tape resources available for those who wish to use them in light of their test scores.

      6. Prepare copies of "Your First Year Budget," found in the Appendix of this book.

      7. Order a copy of "The Pre-Marital Communication Inventory" by Millard J. Bienvenu, Sr., Northwestern State University of Louisiana, Natchitoches, Louisiana 71457. Upon receiving a copy, decide if you want to use these for the session.

5.
1. Prepare copies of the "Finances Questionnaire," found in the Appendix of this book.
2. Prepare transparencies.
3. Duplicate material on in-laws, found in the Appendix.
4. Remind the speaker for this session.

6.
1. Have three couples ready to share at this meeting.
2. Prepare tape or transparency of the wedding vows.
3. Have copies of *The Living Marriage* available.

Prior to the first session couples should receive their copies of *Before You Say I Do*. Ask them to bring them with them each time. The reading schedule is as follows:
1. Prior to the first session, complete chapter 1.
2. Prior to the second session, complete chapters 5 and 10.
3. Prior to the third session, complete chapters 2 and 4.
4. Prior to the fourth session, complete chapters 6 and 7.
5. Prior to the fifth session, complete chapters 9 and 11.
6. Prior to the sixth session, complete chapter 8.

Ask each couple to complete chapters 3 and 12 for devotions together on their honeymoon.

The Interview Preceding Group Counseling

Meet with each couple three to four weeks before the first session. Use this as a time to get better acquainted and to lay a foundation for the series. You may use some of the questions and ideas from session one or from the portion of this book that deals with the initial interview in the individual counseling. In addition, listed here are some simple background questions that you can use with each couple. This get-acquainted meeting is a time to explore each individual's commitment to Jesus Christ and to ascertain his spiritual level and growth.

What do you think marriage is? (Let one answer; then ask the other partner whether he or she can add to the first answer.)

How long have you been going together?

Since you've been going together, what has it been like?

What types of families do you come from?

Are your families basically alike?

How do you get along with each other's parents?

Will the wife work after you get married?

How would you like your marriage relationship to be different from your parents'?

Are you running into any roadblocks as you plan for your marriage ceremony? (Ask both partners.)

DESCRIPTION OF THE ACTIVITY
SESSION 1

5 minutes

1. *All together.*

Introduction by the session leader: Share background information about yourself; then share the purpose of premarital counseling:

a. to help a couple evaluate their own relationship,
b. to form realistic expectations for marriage,
c. to correct inaccurate attitudes and beliefs about marriage,
d. to develop proper habits of thinking and skills of communicating that will enrich the marriage,
e. to gain information about sex, marriage roles, in-laws, finances, and the spiritual relationship so this information can be translated into practice.

Structure and Content: Explain the details of the program to the participants. There will be six sessions, two and three-quarters hours in length, with a fifteen-minute break in the middle of each session. There will be homework between sessions averaging three to five hours a week, depending upon the individual.

Let couples know that there will be adequate time for questions, and that there is nothing that cannot be discussed or asked during the series. If any individuals or couples would like to meet individually with the leader, they may ask for an appointment.

15 minutes

2. *Small groups.*

The purpose of this activity is to get acquainted. Ask class members to form groups of three or four, depending upon how many there are, so the groups are the same size.

Ask members to number off in their group. Then start with the highest number in each group. Each person has two minutes in which to tell about him or herself. Each explains: This is what you need to know about me in order to understand me. At the end of two minutes, the rest of the group can ask questions. Then another member shares and the entire process is repeated until every person has been through the experience.

As the leader, watch the time for everyone. When the activity ends, ask how people felt as they were going through the process. Ask for several to share insights they learned about one another during this procedure.

45 minutes

3. *All together.*

Attitudes toward marriage: Ask the members to complete the following sentences (1-6, and to state "agree" or "disagree" to number 7. They should write their answers on a piece of paper.

  a. Marriage is . . .
  b. Men are . . .
  c. Sex is . . .
  d. My attitudes toward marriage have been shaped by . . .
  e. In marriage a man is . . .
  f. In marriage a woman is . . .
  g. Agree or disagree with this statement: Marriage is a contract.

Show the film *When's the Big Day?* After the film, have students form small groups of three or four persons for a ten-minute discussion; then have the total group discuss the film. Use these questions both times: What attitudes toward marriage did you see in the film? What could be done to correct these attitudes? You may also want to use some of the questions that come with the discussion guide for the film. Put the questions on the chalkboard or on a transparency.

Ask members to look at some of their own attitudes as expressed by the sentence completion and agree-disagree they worked on before the film. Discuss with the whole group the question, Where have you received your attitudes toward marriage?

25 minutes

4. *Small groups.*

Discuss the following questions in small groups of four to six. Put the questions on the chalkboard or make a transparency.

1. What do you hope to get out of your marriage that you would not get if you remain single?
2. Formulate your own definition of marriage.
3. What is the difference between love and infatuation? How can you be sure?
4. What kind of love is it necessary to have before you marry that other individual?

25 minutes

5. *All together—teaching session.*

Take five minutes for brief summaries of what the groups decided. Then take twenty minutes for your teaching, using the following material and suggestions:

a. Share a few of your own ideas of what a person should receive from marriage.
b. Using an overhead projector, show the transparency on the differences between mature love and immature love (or infatuation). You will find this material in the Appendix. Read to them "The Romantic Fallacy."
c. Share the two definitions of love on a transparency ("Real love is" and "Love is a feeling." These are on one sheet in the Appendix.) You may want to amplify these definitions. They are discussed on the tape that will be used next.

    d. Use the tape from the series "Enriching Your Marriage." Find the section near the beginning of the tape where the speaker discusses the definition of marriage. Use this definition on the overhead as the speaker reads it. Take down the transparency during the portion of the message when the speaker is sharing his testimony about his retarded son. This way the class can give their full attention to the testimony being given. Reproduce the definition so class members can take it with them. It is in the Appendix.

Ask the couples to listen to the remainder of the tape series together during the week.

15-20 minutes

6. *Meet as couples, face to face.*

Have the couples discuss the following questions. Ask them to be sure they discuss all of these questions. Put these on the chalkboard or a transparency.

    a. Of how many models of a good marriage are you aware?
    b. What makes these marriages good?
    c. What will you do to make your marriage different from poor marriages? (Some examples might be: building one another's self-esteem, setting goals, actively pursuing activities that would build the marriage such as reading books, attending seminars, keeping lines of communication open, continuing to grow as an individual, and encouraging your partner to grow.)
    d. When is a person ready for marriage?

10-15 minutes

7. *All together—summary lecture.*

During this time share the marriageability traits. These are discussed in detail in the earlier portion of this book in chapter 2.

5 minutes

8. *All together—summary and closing.*

Assign homework:

    a. Ask each person to list ten goals that he or she has for

marriage. They should do this without discussion and bring these to the next session. This could be completed in the appropriate section of the *Before You Say I Do* manual.

b. Distribute the "Marriage Expectation Inventory for Engaged Couples" and the "Sex Knowledge Inventory," form Y. Ask them to complete these individually.

c. Distribute the book *Communication—Key to Your Marriage* and ask them to read and complete the first chapter for this week. The remainder of the book should be completed by the end of the course.

d. Distribute a copy of "Love Dies" by David Knox to each couple. Ask them to read this together during the week. It is in the Appendix.

e. Distribute copies of the in-law form to each couple. Each person receives two since each mother and father completes one. These as well as the letter described earlier in this book are to be sent to you within two weeks.

SESSION 2

10 minutes

1. *All together.*

Provide the "Sex Knowledge Inventory" answer sheets and have them take these with them when the session is over so they can grade their own tests. Ask each couple to share the goals that they wrote for their marriage. Allow three minutes for this. Then ask the group to share what they believe are the most important goals that they devised.

20-25 minutes

2. *Couples together.*

Ask each couple to combine their lists of individual goals into one list.

a. Have them choose the four most important goals.

b. Have them develop the plan and steps necessary to achieve these goals. If possible have them set some target dates for accomplishing the goals. Emphasize the fact that goal setting is the first step, but it is most important to develop a plan to follow in order to attain the goal.

25 minutes

3. *Individuals, then couples face to face.*

"Your Role Concepts Comparison": Ask them to complete this form, which is found in *Before You Say I Do.*

   a. Have each person answer the questions according to his or her own belief.
   b. Ask them to indicate next to each question the source for their own belief. Who or what influenced them? For example, parents, friends, pastor, the Bible, or they thought it up.
   c. Then ask them to answer in the way they think their fiancé would answer.
   d. Ask the couples to sit face to face and discuss their answers. Ask the men to start by picking one statement and saying, "This is how I answered, and this is how I think you answered the statement." Then they should proceed to discuss their answers. When a couple has finished the discussion of one statement, the woman should select the next one, using the same procedure.

20 minutes

4. *All together.*

Ask for reactions and questions concerning the statements of the role comparison sheet. There will be many varied opinions and questions from the group. Be sure you have read over these statements carefully and have thought through your own response. Some members may ask about the woman working or having a career. If not, you may want to bring up the question and share the information from the Appendix. This is titled "Husband-Wife Roles in the 20th Century" and "How Does a Couple Try to Resolve Role Confusion?"

5. *Small groups.*

"Conflicts in Marriage Case Studies": Have the couples meet in groups of two or three couples. Distribute a copy of the case study sheet to each one. Ask them to spend a few moments on two or three of the cases that are most interesting to each of them. Ask them to decide how they would solve these case problems. During the last five minutes, ask for suggestions. The case studies are in the Appendix.

15 minutes

6. *Face to face: then all together.*

Have couples sit face to face and work out the principles and procedures they will follow in handling conflict in their upcoming marriage. During the last five minutes, have the group share insights.

25 minutes

7. *Individuals, then groups of four without partners.*

Ask each person to write answers to these questions:

a. Why are you getting married now? Give eight indications as to why this is the time of your life to marry.
b. Why are you marrying this person? Give at least eight reasons.

As they meet in the groups, each person should take three minutes to share his or her answers; then the others can ask questions for two minutes. Encourage members to share their answers with their fiancé after the session.

5-10 minutes

8. *All together—summary and closing.*

Assignment: Distribute the "Taylor-Johnson Temperament Analysis." Give each person one test booklet and two answer sheets. Ask members to answer the test questions as they see themselves and as they see their fiancé. See chapter 4 of this book for information on the T-JTA.

Distribute the Wheats' *Intended for Pleasure* and the cassette series by Dr. Wheat. Ask members to read this book during the next week and listen to the tape.

Suggest that couples spend some time sharing answers from the "Marriage Expectation Inventory for Engaged Couples." Have them think about questions or fears they have about their forthcoming marriage.

Close in prayer.

SESSION 3

5 minutes

1. *All together.*

Have everyone turn in their T-JTA on themselves and their fiancé. Ask if there are any questions related to the "Marriage Expectation Inventory for Engaged Couples."

25 minutes

2. *All together.*

Show the film *Johnny Lingo.* You can order it from many Christian or secular film distributors or from Augsburg Films, 3224 Beverly Blvd., Los Angeles, Calif. 90057. This is an outstanding film on building self-esteem.

20 minutes

3. *Large or small groups.*

If you have a large group for this series, have six or seven sit in the center of the room and discuss the questions while the others listen. If this is a smaller group have them discuss it together or in groups of three.

Discussion questions: Put these questions on the chalkboard or make a transparency.

    a. What can a person do to build self-esteem in his or her mate?
    b. What are the most common ways to destroy self-esteem?
    c. What has helped you the most to feel worthwhile?
    d. How is a person likely to act or respond when he or she does not like himself or herself?

During the last five minutes, have each individual write down what he or she can do to build self-esteem in his or her partner. Ask them not to share this but to put it into practice.

30 minutes

4. *All together.*

Give a 3 × 5 card to every person. Ask them to write down any questions or fears that they have about marriage. They may ask about anything; you may want to mention or suggest some topic areas. For example: sex, contraception, unwanted pregnancy, pain during intercourse, premature ejaculation, difference in the intensity of the sex drive, losing interest in each other, the morality of oral sex, deviant sex behavior, scriptural teaching on sex, children, or divorce. Do not have members put their names on the cards. Collect the cards.

Start off the discussion by raising the questions, To what extent should a Christian couple be involved sexually prior to marriage? How can a person deal with guilt if going too far prior to marriage? See the Appendix for "God's Word: Wait Until Marriage." You may want to make this into a transparency to use at this point.

Now read some of the questions that the members wrote. Allow the group to discuss the questions and you can add or correct information as needed.

For your own preparation you could listen to the tape series that will be distributed at the close of this session; you may also want to listen to the series entitled "Sex and the Bible" by H. Norman Wright, from Christian Marriage Enrichment, 8000 E. Girard, Denver, Colorado 80231. Read Dwight H. Small's book *Christian: Celebrate Your Sexuality*, published by Revell, or *Thank God for Sex* by Harry Hollis, Jr., Broadman.

If this portion of the session takes longer than thirty minutes, do not cut it short. These are important questions. Adjust your schedule by reducing the times for 5 and 6; or have 6 later, or as a homework assignment.

15 minutes

5. *Small groups.*

Have the couples discuss the following questions:

   a. How were feelings of love, warmth, and tenderness shown in your home as you were growing up?
   b. How would you like to have feelings of love, warmth, and tenderness shown to you in public and in your home?

15 minutes

6. *Face to face.*

List the following questions on a transparency and have members write their answers. Then ask couples to sit face to face, share their answers, and work out any differences they might have.

    a. Do you like sympathy and attention when you are ill?

    b. Generally, do you enjoy the companionship of the opposite sex as much, or more, than your own? After you are married, do you think you will look at members of the opposite sex?

    c. How much praise do you feel you need?

    d. Do you like your future spouse's friends?

    e. Do you have many friends?

    f. How will you select friends after you are married?

    g. What activities do you desire to do together and apart after marriage?

40 minutes

7. *Small groups.*

Ask groups of four to six to work out ten Scriptures that they feel a married couple should base their marriage upon. See *The Living Marriage* for suggestions. Ask them not to select the traditional passages such as Ephesians 5, 1 Peter 3, 1 Corinthians 13, or Proverbs 31. Those passages are important, and we take it for granted that they would be a part of a couple's life. The idea here is to come up with some Scriptures not always associated with marriage.

During the last fifteen minutes, show Ephesians 4:2, Amplified version, on a transparency. Ask members to individually visualize or describe what they would do to put that passage into practice in their married life. Ask them to write down their suggestions and then have several share these with the group.

5 minutes

8. *All together.*

Closing: Ask everyone to continue reading the book, *Communication—Key to Your Marriage.* Read chapters 2 through 5 before next time. Give each couple a set of the tapes "Sex Problems and Sex Technique in Marriage" by Dr. Ed Wheat. (They are to be returned to you later.) Ask them to set aside time during the week to listen to the tapes together. Explain that this is a very frank, detailed presentation from a Christian medical doctor. When you preview these tapes yourself, decide whether you will suggest that couples listen just to the first one, or to both.

Close with prayer.

SESSION 4

1 hour and 20 minutes

1. *All together.*

Distribute the session 4 "What Is Your Opinion" agree-disagree sheet from the Appendix to each class member. Provide pencils. After the sheets have been distributed, give the following instructions:

Each of you has been given an agree-disagree sheet. On the sheet you will find several statements concerning the specifics of the marriage relationship. I would like each of you (without talking with anyone else) to read each statement and decide whether you agree or disagree with it as it is presented there. If you agree place a check mark in the blank under "agree." If you disagree place a check in the blank marked "disagree." You will be given sufficient time to answer the statements. Please work individually and as quickly as possible.

Give the class enough time to complete their work. When everyone has finished, thank them for completing the sheet. Then ask all those who agreed with statement 1 to raise their hands. Then ask how many of them disagreed with that statement. Proceed to statement 2 and ask how many agreed and how many disagreed. Do this for each of the agree-disagree statements without stopping to discuss any of the statements.

Give members seven minutes to discuss their response in small groups of three.

You will need one hour for the tape presentation. Listen to the tape entitled "Communication Is the Key" from the series "Communication—Key to Your Marriage." Make an overhead transparency or a chart of the main points and Scriptures. You may want to make a fill-in outline so the participants could copy down the main points. A number of these points will be reinforced by their continued reading in the communication book.

Following the tape show this statement on the overhead: "What do you think about this? Most problems in communication occur because each person communicates on a different level than the other. The longer a couple is married the more they learn what *not* to talk about."

Ask, "In light of the five levels of communication in your reading during the past week, what level do you communicate on? (Refer to pages 67 and 68 of *Communication—Key to Your Marriage*.) Is there a difference in your level as compared with your fiancé's? Are there things now that you hesitate to talk about?" (You may want to read these five levels to them.) Take your break at this time and have them consider these questions. They may want to bring these up again later.

Note: You may want to use the "Premarital Communication Inventory." See the Advance Preparation Section.

30 minutes

2. *All together.*

Explain the background and scope of the "Taylor-Johnson Temperament Analysis" test. Define the traits. You may want to have a large blow-up of the T-JTA profile. This is available from the publishers of the test; one is now available with an acetate so you can draw on it. (See address in the Advance Preparation Section.)

Ask each person to predict his or her own profile. Be sure to explain the mid-scores and the attitude score. After each one has predicted his or her own score, return the completed profiles so they can see the result of their tests.

Allow time for questions. Discuss the potential interrelationships of trait scores on a couple's profile and how these might affect the marriage.

Note: You will probably have some profiles which will indicate that the person needs further counseling on an individual basis. Be sure that you indicate that this is available. You may ask individuals in for counseling or if you see too many scores in the white area of the test or if you see great differences in the couples' scores and their perception of one another.

Be sure you have available many of the books and tape resources suggested for improving any of the scores. Note the materials recommended under the listing of T-JTA resources and Scriptures. Refer to the Appendix for this listing.

25 minutes

3. *Small groups.*

This is a time for a discussion of some of the trait scores, such as:

    a. How can a person become less nervous?

    b. How should a person handle hostility constructively?

    c. In what ways could impulsiveness become detrimental?

    d. How could self-discipline stabilize a marriage?

    e. Is the submission talked about on this test the same kind of submission discussed in the Scriptures?

    f. What effect would a high score in subjectivity have upon the marriage?

Have the members discuss how they feel about their own scores and the way they saw their fiancé's. Have them share what they would like to change, and have the members in the group suggest ways to change or improve.

15 minutes

4. *All together.*

Take questions and reactions at this point from the entire group. Suggest reading and tape material for each trait's improvement.

Spend some time taking prayer requests; close this meeting with a time of concentrated prayer. Let members know again that you or other pastoral staff are available for individual discussion of the test.

Homework assignment: Have each couple work out a budget. Distribute a copy of "Your First Year Budget." See Appendix.

Ask the members to find out the cost of items normally taken care of by the other partner; for example, the women could find out how much it would cost to buy a set of tires and have a car lubricated. Ask men to find out the cost of women's clothing, food, baby items, or furniture. If anyone still lives at home, have him or her volunteer to do the grocery shopping for the next week. This will be valuable experience.

SESSION 5

20 minutes

1. *All together.*

This time should be spent in an open discussion using some of the following questions:

- a. Were you aware of what things cost today? Were you surprised?
- b. Have you ever used a budget before? How can you control spending of money that is not budgeted?
- c. Should marriage partners have an allowance that they do not have to account for? Why or why not?
- d. Who should take responsibility of working out the budget and paying the bills? Why? Where does the concept of spiritual gifts come into play here?

20 minutes

2. *Individuals, then couples, face to face.*

Distribute a copy of the "Finances Questionnaire." Have each person complete it; then ask the couples to sit face to face and discuss the various items.

45 minutes

3. *All together.*

This portion of the meeting is given to a special speaker that you have invited. This should be a Christian businessman or accountant who can give specific and practical guidelines on making and living within a budget. Be very selective when you choose this person; ask him or her to give as many helpful hints as possible during the forty-five minutes. If this person represents a company or organization, let him or her know that this is a teaching situation, not a promotional time.

25 minutes

4. *Groups of three couples.*

Place the following questions on an overhead transparency. Ask the couples to discuss as many as possible in the time allotted.

a. When should you spend more to get quality, and when can you skimp on quality in order to save? Discuss the following: car (new or used; "transportation" or "sports"); housing (rent or buy); furniture (mattress, stove, refrigerator, sofa, stereo, etc.); food (steak, casseroles, leftovers); wearing apparel (clothes, shoes, cosmetics); dishes and silverware; gifts (to your mate, to others).

b. What type of vacation do you want? (Camping or a Caribbean cruise?) How much will it cost? How will you save for it? How often will you take a vacation?

c. What kind of honeymoon will you take? How much will it cost? How will you pay for it?

d. How was money handled in each of your families? What attitudes regarding money do you bring to your marriage? What were considered luxuries, what necessities?

e. What types of charge accounts will you have (gasoline, department store, bank card)? What amount of money would each partner feel comfortable owing on charge accounts? Will charge accounts be used regularly or only for emergencies?

f. What do you think about borrowing money from relatives?

g. What are your financial goals?

h. How soon will you attempt to buy furniture? What type (expensive, fix-it-yourself, or in-between)? How much will you spend? What major appliances will you buy? How soon? How much will you spend?

i. What things do you consider necessities or luxuries?

5-10 minutes

5. *All together.*

The group leader should give information about the following:

a. It is important to establish good credit (for major expenditures as a house, car, having a baby, or emergencies).

b. What you pay in gasoline tax is deductible on your income tax, and charging gas is a good way to keep track of it. Or you can keep a record of mileage driven during the year and use government gas tax tables to estimate taxes paid.

c. Do you know that utility companies usually require a

deposit in order to begin service? (Sometimes $25 to $50 each!)

d. Do you know where to borrow money? There is a great difference in what finance charge you will have to pay. Usually a credit union is best, a bank is next, and a "mouse house" (finance company) worst.

e. Your application for a marriage license is public record. Many firms use the list of marriage license applicants as a list of new prospects. Expect to be barraged by mail, telephone, and door-to-door solicitation. Can you say, "NO!"?

f. Beware the door-to-door salesman. Your unborn child does not need a complete encyclopedia set!

g. Any sale made at your home in California may be canceled if written notice is mailed to the company within three days of the sale. Other states may have this law, too.

30 minutes

6. *Individuals, then all together.*

The remaining time should be spent looking at attitudes toward in-laws and sharing principles to follow in dealing with in-laws. Make a transparency of the following questions for a brief agree-disagree sheet.

Agree	Disagree	Statement
_____	_____	1. If you have any difficulties in your own marriage, it might be helpful to get advice from your parents.
_____	_____	2. Most in-law problems come from the mother-in-law, not the father-in-law.
_____	_____	3. You should visit or call one set of parents just as much as the other.
_____	_____	4. It might be best at the start of the marriage to let parents and in-laws know that you would like to learn on your own and would appreciate not receiving any advice.
_____	_____	5. If a wife has a disagreement with his mother, the husband should stay out of the discussion and let them work it out.

Please answer this question: Where and how do you want to spend your first Thanksgiving and Christmas?

Follow the usual procedure for an agree-disagree sheet, but this time have a five- to ten-minute discussion. Then complete this session by sharing the principles of "Dealing with In-laws" from Landis and Landis and Lobenz and Blackburn. Make a transparency of these items and use this for a lecture base for your presentation. Duplicate a copy of the material and give to each couple. This material is found in the Appendix. Also read over the adapted material from David Mace as that will help your presentation. This material has been adapted from his book *We Can Have Better Marriages If We Really Want Them.* You may want to read this material in the original.

Distribute the in-law letters and forms that you have received. Suggest that the couples read and discuss these together following the session.

3 minutes

7. *Close.*

Suggest that each couple think of one positive act they could perform during this coming week for each set of parents. Ask them to continue reading *Communication—Key to Your Marriage* and other books or resources they might be using in conjunction with their T-JTA. Ask them to plan at least one session together this week for Bible study and prayer. Suggest J. Allan Pederson's excellent workbook *Two Become One* published by Tyndale and available in Christian bookstores. This would give them the format and structure that they might be looking for.

Close in prayer.

Session 6

5 minutes

1. *All together.*

Ask the couples to share their reactions and feelings about their Bible study and praying together. Be willing to share some of your own feelings and insights with them.

15 minutes

2. *Groups of two or three couples.*

Discussion question: What provision are you making for continuing your own spiritual growth? Ask the couples to discuss this together. Ask them also to discuss these questions:

a. Should a couple pray and study the Scriptures together every day?
b. Who decides what church they attend and how often?

30 minutes

3. *Two groups and then all together.*

Ask the women to meet in a group and the men to meet in a group. Each group is to discuss, How will I contribute to my partner's spiritual growth? After fifteen minutes, ask each group to share their ideas with the total group.

As group leader you may want to make some of the following suggestions:

a. Individual study of the same passage, then share findings together.
b. Use a Bible study guide or commentary, such as *Barclay's Daily Study Bible* or the *Aldersgate Adult Bible Study material*. (This Free Methodist material is inductive in approach.)
c. Use a concordance for a topical study.
d. Listen to tapes or use Bible studies on family topics.
e. Play the "Ungame" or use the game's Christian and Bible study cards as discussion topics. (For information on the game and the Bible study cards, write to Christian Marriage Enrichment, 8000 E. Girard, Suite 602, Denver, CO 80231).
f. Each morning you might ask each other what you could pray for during that day; then have a time of sharing together, and close by reading 1 Samuel 12:23.

45 minutes to one hour

4. *All together.*

Now three married couples you have selected will share insights they have learned over the years. Select one couple that has been married a few years, another married ten to twenty years, and one who has been married more than twenty years. Select couples who have something to offer and can be open, honest, and responsive.

Let the couples know that they will be asked all kinds of questions. Ask each couple to share specifically what Jesus Christ has meant in their marriage and how they have grown spiritually and helped each other to grow during their marriage. Let the class members know that they can ask any questions that they would like to have answered at this time.

10 minutes

5. *Groups of three individuals.*

It is important to introduce the topic of child rearing and discipline so the couples will plan to equip themselves well before having children. Ask them to discuss the following questions:

a. How did your parents discipline you?
b. How do you feel about it now?
c. Would you do things the same or differently?
d. If differently, how do you know that you will be able to do it differently?

5 minutes

6. *All together.*

Just as it requires study and learning to become skilled craftsmen, it requires study and learning to become a good parent. Many people want to rear their own children differently than they were reared. However, most people revert to the same procedures their parents used unless the couple puts forth an effort to learn new procedure and principles.

Suggest to the members that before they have children they could do the following:

a. Spend time with small children so they can receive some firsthand experience.
b. Consider working in the church's nursery or two-year-old department for three months; this could be an education in itself!
c. Listen to the series of tapes by the Reverend Charles R. Swindoll on parent-child relationships. Order from the First

Evangelical Free Church, 642 W. Malvern, Fullerton, California 92632. Also listen to *The Family in Today's Society*, available from your Christian bookstore or from Herald Press, Scottdale, Pennsylvania 15683.

  d. Read the following books (available from Christian bookstores):

  1) *Help! I'm a Parent*, by S. Bruce Narramore
  2) *Your Child's Self-Esteem*, by Dorothy Briggs
  3) *Hide or Seek*, by James Dobson
  4) *The Concordia Sex Education Series*.
  5) *Preparing for Parenthood* by Marvin N. Inmon and H. Norman Wright (Ventura, Cal.: Gospel Light, Regal, 1980).

20 minutes

7. *Men in groups and women in groups.*

Make a transparency or tape recording of the sample vows in the Appendix. Show or play this for the group. With the help of the group, each person should write, in everyday language, what he or she wants to promise to his or her partner. Each person's vows may be different from others in the group, but each may benefit from sharing ideas.

10 minutes

8. *Couples face to face.*

The couples should read their vows to each other and discuss any part that is not clear. They may share their feelings about the promises they have received and given. Are the promises realistic?

Close session with couples praying together in small groups.

As your wedding gift to them, give each couple a copy of *The Living Marriage*, published by Revell or *Into the High Country* by H. Norman Wright. Encourage them not to read this together until their honeymoon, so they could use it as the first devotional study of their married life.

Appendix

Immature Love

1. Love is born at first sight and will conquer all.

2. Love demands exclusive attention and devotion, and is jealous of outsiders.

3. Love is characterized by exploitation and direct need gratification.

4. Love is built upon physical attraction and sexual gratification. Sex often dominates the relationship.

5. Love is static and egocentric. Change is sought in the partner in order to satisfy one's own needs and desires.

6. Love is romanticized. The couple does not face reality or is frightened by it.

Mature Love

1. Love is a developing relationship and deepens with realistically shared experiences.

2. Love is built upon self-acceptance and is shared unselfishly with others.

3. Love seeks to aid and strengthen the loved one without striving for recompense.

4. Love includes sexual satisfaction, but not to the exclusion of sharing in other areas of life.

5. Love is growing and developing reality. Love expands to include the growth and creativity of the loved one.

6. Love enhances reality and makes the partners more complete and adequate persons.

199

THE ROMANTIC FALLACY[2]

First, romance results in such distortions of personality that after marriage the two people can never fulfill the roles that they expect of each other. Second, romance so idealizes marriage and even sex that when the day-to-day experiences of marriage are encountered there must be disillusionment involved. Third, the romantic complex is so short-sighted that the pre-marital relationship is conducted almost entirely on the emotional level and consequently such problems as temperamental or value differences, religious or cultural, or health problems are never considered. Fourth, romance develops such a false ecstasy that there is implied in courtship a promise of a kind of happiness which could never be maintained during the realities of married life. Fifth, romance is such an escape from the negative aspects of personality to the extent that their repression obscures the real person. Later in marriage these negative factors in marital adjustment are bound to appear, and they do so in far greater detail and far more importantly simply because they were not evident earlier. Sixth, people engrossed in romance seem to be prohibited from wise planning for the basic needs of the future even to the extent of failing to discuss the significant problems of early marriage.

It is difficult to know how pervasive the romantic fallacy really is. I suspect that it creates the greatest havoc with high school seniors or that half of the population who are married before they are twenty years old. Nevertheless, even in a college or young adult population, one constantly finds as a final criterion for marriage the question of being in love. This is due to the distortion of the meaning of a true companionship in marriage by the press, by the magazines, and by cultural impact upon the last two or three generations. The result is that more serious and sober aspects of marital choice and marital expectations are not only neglected but sometimes ridiculed.

A Definition of Marriage

A Christian marriage is a total commitment of two people to the Person of Jesus Christ and to one another. It is a commitment in which there is no holding back of anything. A Christian marriage is similar to a solvent, a freeing up of the man and woman to be themselves and become all that God intends for them to become. Marriage is the refining process that God will use to have us develop into the man or woman he wants us to be.

LOVE DIES[3]

Love feelings are not "built in" but come from learned social responses, for example, a smile, a touch, a laugh. Most of the things that make us feel good are incorporated into our cultural system of dating and courtship; we treat the other person very courteously, smile a lot, try to be pleasant, avoid saying offensive things, dress to look attractive, use best manners, and perhaps dine on food and enjoy entertainment that takes us beyond our budget. More important, all of these pleasurable features appear against a background of escalating physical stimulation or sexual excitement. Indeed, we have a social interaction in which one's dating partner is paired with the widest possible range of pleasurable sensations and activities. (Bartz and Rasor, 1972, used by permission.)

Consider this explanation of love in your dating relationship. Think about someone you just met. It is not possible for this person to elicit love feelings in you unless you have already shared a number of pleasurable experiences (e.g., eating together, seeing movies together, talking together). The "love at first sight" experience is the result of seeing someone whose features (eyes, face, body type) have already been paired with love feelings. For example, it would be difficult for you to fall romantically in love with someone three times your age. This love possibility with an elderly person is reduced because you have not experienced love (romantic) feelings with someone that age nor have you been taught to expect love feelings. The experience of love requires a cultural readiness.

The behaviors which cause love feelings must be reinforced to be maintained. This implies that during a developing relationship, couples have a high frequency of reinforcing each other for appropriate behavior. This results in the partner continuing the desired behavior which results in the continuation of love feelings. If you want your partner to continue to engage in behavior which you define as desirable, you must reinforce or reward that behavior.

Love dies when partners spend little time together and stop sharing activities that are mutually enjoyable. . . . As a test . . . , identify an unhappy couple you know and specify how much time they spend together engaging in enjoyable behavior. Contrast this with a couple you define as being in love and observe the amount of time they spend in mutually enjoyable activities. Love can be created or destroyed by pairing or failing to pair the partner with pleasurable activities over time.

The death of love also results from failure on the part of both partners to reinforce appropriate behavior in each other. For example, smiling, caressing, complimenting, spending time together, and helping with the baby are behaviors in marriage that may not be reinforced. When these behaviors are no longer reinforced, they will stop. If your partner stops doing things that you like, your love feelings will disappear. It is important that you reinforce your partner for positive behavior (so that the behavior will continue) to insure that there is a continued basis for your love feelings.

In summary, love is a function of sharing pleasurable activities with each other over time, reinforcing your partner, and being reinforced by your partner for appropriate behavior. When partners stop spending time with each other in pleasurable mutual activities and stop reinforcing each other for appropriate behavior, love dies.

How Does a Couple Try to Resolve Role Confusion?

In recent studies, husband and wife role differences are the result of "balance of power" in the marriage. The "sources of power are in the comparative resources which the husband and wife bring to the marriage." "A resource may be designated as anything that one partner may make available to the other, helping the other satisfy his needs or attain his goals. The balance of power will be on the side of that partner who contributes the greater resources to the marriage." In the past, that power was allocated to the one with the greater physical strength.

THERE ARE SEVEN BASES OF FAMILY POWER:

1. Personalities of spouses: It might be assumed that the more

Your Role Concepts Comparison[4]

What do you believe about your role in marriage?

Answer Key:
1. Strongly agree
2. Mildly agree
3. Not sure
4. Mildly disagree
5. Strongly disagree

Wife					Statement	Husband				
1	2	3	4	5	The husband is the head of the home.	1	2	3	4	5
1	2	3	4	5	The wife should not be employed outside of the home.	1	2	3	4	5
1	2	3	4	5	The husband should help regularly with the dishes.	1	2	3	4	5
1	2	3	4	5	The wife has the greater responsibility for the children.	1	2	3	4	5
1	2	3	4	5	Money that the wife earns is her money.	1	2	3	4	5
1	2	3	4	5	The husband should have at least one night a week out with his friends.	1	2	3	4	5
1	2	3	4	5	The wife should always be the one to cook.	1	2	3	4	5
1	2	3	4	5	The husband's responsibility is to his job and the wife's responsibility is to the home and children.	1	2	3	4	5
1	2	3	4	5	Money can best be handled through a joint checking account.	1	2	3	4	5
1	2	3	4	5	Marriage is a 50-50 proposition.	1	2	3	4	5
1	2	3	4	5	Major decisions should be made by the husband in case of an impasse.	1	2	3	4	5
1	2	3	4	5	The husband should babysit one night a week so the wife can get away and do what she wants.	1	2	3	4	5
1	2	3	4	5	A couple should spend their recreation leisure activities with one another.	1	2	3	4	5
1	2	3	4	5	It is all right for the wife to initiate love-making with her husband.	1	2	3	4	5

Wife					Statement	Husband				
1	2	3	4	5	The husband and wife should plan the budget and manage money matters together.	1	2	3	4	5
1	2	3	4	5	Neither the husband nor the wife should purchase an item costing over ~~fifteen~~ 20 dollars without consulting the other.	1	2	3	4	5
1	2	3	4	5	The father is the one responsible for disciplining the children.	1	2	3	4	5
1	2	3	4	5	A wife who has special talent should have a career.	1	2	3	4	5
1	2	3	4	5	It is the wife's responsibility to have the house neat and clean.	1	2	3	4	5
1	2	3	4	5	The husband should take his wife out somewhere twice a month.	1	2	3	4	5
1	2	3	4	5	The wife is just as responsible for the children's discipline as the husband.	1	2	3	4	5
1	2	3	4	5	It is the husband's job to do the yard work.	1	2	3	4	5
1	2	3	4	5	The mother should be the teacher of values to the children.	1	2	3	4	5
1	2	3	4	5	Women are more emotional than men.	1	2	3	4	5
1	2	3	4	5	Children should be allowed to help plan family activities.	1	2	3	4	5
1	2	3	4	5	Children develop better in a home with parents who are strict disciplinarians.	1	2	3	4	5
1	2	3	4	5	The wife should always obey what her husband asks her to do.	1	2	3	4	5
1	2	3	4	5	The husband should decide which areas each should be responsible for.	1	2	3	4	5
1	2	3	4	5	Neither husband nor wife should bring their parents into the home to live.	1	2	3	4	5

dominant personality would wield the greater power in marriage. However, studies show that this is more valid with the dominant male than the female.

2. The relative age of spouses: When there is a large difference in age, the scale is tipped in favor of the older spouse, usually the husband.

3. The relative education of spouses: Generally the spouse with the higher educational level has more influence in the marriage than he or she would otherwise have. Influence seems particularly noticeable when one mate is college educated.

4. The employment status of the wife: Power wielded by additional income is probably the decision factor. The full-time working wife has the most influence in family decisions. Other studies show the housewife exerts more influence. More study is needed in this area.

5. The occupational status of husband: This has a great deal to do with his status in the home. Most wives will recognize they owe their status to the good position of their husbands. Therefore, they will be more dependent, even though they may be well-educated women. In lower class situations where the wife's income is essential to family welfare, the husband's bargaining power is not as great.

6. The presence and number of children in the family: It has been demonstrated that childless couples tend to be more equalitarian than couples with children. The more children in the family, the more influence the husband has.

7. The stage in the family cycle: In early years of marriage there is a more equalitarian pattern. With the coming of children, the husband seems to dominate. Once children leave and there is the empty nest, very few wives are dominated by their husbands. This shows that the balance of power shifts throughout a marriage.

Husband-Wife Roles in the Twentieth Century

One of the greatest areas of adjustments, change, and concern in today's marriages revolves around the roles of the husband and wife.

In our American culture an assumption has existed concerning sex-role distinctions and definitions. For example, traditionally expressive behavior has been designated to women and instrumental behavior to men. But is this actually true? The patterns of interaction within marriage are not always that clear-cut nor are the roles that segregated. We have certain expectations and stereotypes for behavior, such as the behavior of a father toward his children. But within this expectation there is tremendous variation because of personality, work, and pressures. Our roles are actually more like stereotypes.

Perhaps as man and woman begin to interact there is some segregation of the roles. But after the relationship develops, the roles begin to drop off and more realistic methods of functioning together are developed.

In most American marriages the husband is still the main income provider, and the wife cares for the children. Both are instrumental roles. And there is little evidence to prove that the woman is the only one involved in emotional expressive behavior. In families with children at home, it is too difficult to have a simple division of roles along instrumental-expressive lines because of the complexity of living together. Each person, whether husband or wife, needs to be instrumental and expressive in his behavior. Actually, husbands who are not emotionally supportive to their wives and affectionate to their children could be disruptive to family life. And wives who do not effectively direct the affairs of the household could also be a disruptive influence to the family.[5]

One of the greatest changes evidenced in today's marriages is that of the working wife or career wife.

The traditional view of the American wife is domestic: she marries early and spends the remainder of her life caring for her children and husband. But that picture has changed. Today half of all girls are married by age twenty-one and by thirty-two the average American woman has her youngest child in school. By forty-five, her children have left home and her life expectancy is seventy-seven.

In February 1974, there were 35 million women in the United States labor force, comprising 45 percent of all women age sixteen and over—up nine percentage points since 1955. Mothers, with children under age three and husbands present, had a labor force participation rate of 29 percent in 1973, about a 100 percent increase since 1960. Wives who worked full time year round in

1972 accounted for a median of nearly 40 percent of family income. There has also been a sharp expansion in the proportion of women heading families and households. In 1973, 6.6 million US families were headed by women. It is projected that by 1980 one in four households will be headed by a woman.[6]

The traditional role of the woman keeping house is unfulfilling to many women and understandably so. In years past the woman not only kept house but was involved in part of the productive labor of an economic enterprise (see Prov. 31). Much of the wife's work and production responsibility was withdrawn from the household, and this exaggerated the division of labor between husband and wife. The trend today toward women's employment outside the home is a logical consequence of moving all of the production out of the home, including the husband's work. In the past the woman's functions could be fulfilled in one location and outside employment was unnecessary.

There are several reasons why wives are drawn into employment outside of the home. Ginzberg and Yohalem in *Educated American Women: Self Portraits* suggest four basic categories of women and their reasons for seeking employment outside the home. The first group are the "planners." These women have had definite goals from a young age and have pursued those goals without allowing anything to deter them. The second group are the "recasters," women who shift their interests, plans, and goals when something else is more desirable. They may have had original ideas about what they wanted to do with their lives but because of some obstacles they settled for another choice. Some of these women simply decided that what they chose in the beginning was not what they wanted so they sought something better.

A third group is the "adapters," highly flexible women. They realize early in adulthood there will be many adjustments and changes. No matter what happens at the various stages of marriage, they are ready to make the adjustment.

The last group is given the title "unsettled." These women may have been at one time in any of the other three categories. But because their plans have not been realized, they now fumble and search for a new style and are still somewhat frustrated.[7]

In addition to the above, other practical reasons for employment enter in. As living costs keep rising, many couples find that both partners must work to make ends meet. The desire to add items to the home, to maintain too high a standard of living, or a belief that the husband cannot provide adequately motivates some wives to work. A common goal of saving money for a child's education sends some wives looking for a job.

The wife's personality is another factor. For many women measuring the soap for the dishwasher, choosing the right cycle on the dryer, or cleaning the living room for the sixth time in a week is not very fulfilling. What happens when all of the children are in school and the wife is well organized? It takes more than soap operas and magazines to provide fulfillment. Outside employment is just one means of fulfillment, however.

In the past, wives were not expected to work. Today society not only accepts working women but in some ways may even expect it. Now the pressure has been reversed. The work ethic must go on, and if wives cannot find enough to do within the home then the ethic pushes them to work outside of the home.

The move toward employment is not without emotional upheaval, however. Wives who are committed to work for achievement goals and who aspire to a career often have anxieties, doubts, occasional feelings of role conflict and guilt. Questions arise such as, Is it really all right to work? Is this best for my family? How am I doing in my profession? Some women actually begin worrying about their own normality when the freedom of choice replaces rigid cultural norms, and they must make their own standards and decisions. Uncertainty about their femininity arises when a career atypical for a woman is chosen.[8]

It will take years for attitudes to change and new roles to be accepted. A recent poll showed that 31 percent of American wives feel that "a woman's ultimate fulfillment in life is the realization of her own personal goals," but 67 percent felt that "a woman's ultimate fulfillment in life is marriage and motherhood." And the majority of the wives rejected the idea of complete equality with their husbands: 60 percent of the wives who did want more from life than a husband and children did not want complete equality with their spouses.[9]

What is the effect of the working wife upon the marriage relationship? The conclusions of research are not that clear-cut. In

[some] families, the wife decreases her housekeeping activities while the husband increases his by performing masculine tasks more unilaterally and helping with more feminine tasks. But in many families conflict arises because of the revised division of labor. It has also been found that the power structure shifts in the direction of the wife who now has a greater voice in major economic decisions and a lesser voice in routine household decisions. Some studies have shown that when both the husband and wife were career oriented, pursuing such goals as law, college teaching, or medicine, husbands did not appear threatened or dominated. But this study also indicated that none of the wives wanted to be more successful than her husband.[10]

A common assumption about working wives is that the couple's amount of interaction will lessen. But again this has not been found to be the case. Some time-consuming leisure activities may be curtailed, but there is still ample interaction and involvement together.

In terms of marital happiness, some findings indicate that there is no difference in the marital adjustment of working and nonworking wives. But what really matters is the husband's attitude toward the wife's employment. Nearly all recent studies show a relationship between a wife's full-time employment and conflict in the marriage, but unfortunately this relationship is not that clear and not that accurately defined. It is apparent that both partners experience more tensions and less companionship in their marriage when the wife works by necessity than by choice. When the wife works only because she wants to, tensions are lower and companionship higher than if the wife chose to stay at home. When the wife works part-time as compared to full-time, the marriages tend to be happier.

One interesting study found that the wife's working is evidently a source of marital conflict. But the added income puts the family on a higher socioeconomic level and this has a positive effect upon the family. These two items balance each other so that the final effect of the wife's employment is really negligible.[11]

Perhaps all of these findings seem confusing and contradictory but what they do indicate is that more extensive studies are needed. It may be too soon to know all of the results, but each couple ought to be aware of some possible effects of the wife's employment. If employment is the couple's choice they must work together to resolve and eliminate detrimental effects upon their relationship.

Because so many wives with small children work, Robert Kelley has suggested ten ideal conditions for this situation.

1. Any career for a woman should offer sufficient financial compensation. The salary should be commensurate with her education and should allow her enough money to pay for child care, housekeeping, and other expenses incurred because of working. If there is insufficient money left over to meet family needs, the position might not be worthwhile.

2. Personal satisfaction should be derived from the career. A combination of fulfillment with challenge and stimulation is necessary as compared with jobs that are simply an energy drain.

3. An adequate mother-substitute must be obtained to take care of the children while the mother is at work. This may be the most difficult condition to fulfill. A reevaluation of the nursery school or individual taking care of the child must be done consistently by both the husband and wife.

4. The employed wife needs the understanding and encouragement of her husband. If this does not occur, not only the marriage but the wife's effectiveness on the job can suffer.

5. A mother who is career oriented should be just as interested in the social, moral, and intellectual development of the children. As a child is entrusted to others during the formative years and especially during the three-to-five-year-old age, the quality of the care and education must be high.

6. An employed wife must balance her life so she has time and energy to give to her husband and children. This may require adjustments at home but also the career might have to be selected with this in mind.

7. In a two-career family, the quality of living should remain high, otherwise working is detrimental. For a home to be dirty, meals poorly planned, with little leisure or family time, the mother's job does not help; it hurts. Good planning and a willingness to work together should keep living at a quality level.

8. A long-range benefit of a wife's career should be the improvement of the marital relationship. This is difficult to achieve and difficult to measure. Perhaps a career can assist a

woman in developing her resources and interests. She may make more effort regarding personal attractiveness than one who is much more restricted.

9. It is possible for the woman to gain increased appreciation for her husband and children as they work to make the home surroundings a place of refuge and comfort. This condition is important for any working wife or husband.

10. Community expectations must be considered since certain areas of the country and certain cities are more open to the newer life-styles than are others. In selecting a community in which to live this ought to be taken into consideration. Positive reinforcement from community and acquaintances can lessen the adjustment difficulties.[12]

Is there any effect upon the children when both mother and father are employed outside of the home? Some alarmist articles imply a picture of increased divorces, messy homes and messy children, and delinquency or emotional disturbances in the children because of the mother working. However, these conditions can also occur when the mother is at home.

In all actuality, the studies appear to be contradictory and somewhat uncertain as to the effect a mother's working has upon the children. If mothers feel guilty about working or dislike their jobs there could be some negative effects upon the children. Other mothers could be so stimulated and thus grow so much personally that they become even better mothers during the time they spend with their children.

There are mixed attitudes toward mothers of preschool children working. It appears that more middle-class mothers who have children of this age would not work as compared with those that must out of economic necessity.

There does appear to be some evidence indicating that the mother's employment affects boys differently than girls. The employment may have a positive effect for the girls and a negative effect for the boys. A few studies indicate that there may be a higher rate of delinquency in middle-class homes where both parents work. Another study indicates that boys are affected negatively when the motives for the mother's working reflects failure on the part of the father as the head of the household. Some studies indicate that boys of working mothers may be more dependent and withdrawn. Girls, on the other hand, may admire their mothers more and develop a more clearly formed self-concept.[13]

There are indications that mothers who are employed have a better adjustment to their children than those who are not employed. They seem to share positive feelings more, use milder methods of discipline, and desire more pleasure from their children. However, employed mothers report more frequent doubts and feelings of inadequacy as parents than nonworking mothers.[14]

CASE STUDIES ON CONFLICTS IN MARRIAGE[15]

1. We've been married eleven weeks, and Frank has just told me that with fall coming on, he is planning four or five nights a month out with the boys, bowling or just doing some talking. He says we both need private lives and our own circle of friends and that I should make similar arrangements.

Now, I can understand occasional nights out, but this planning to be apart bothers me. I married him to be with him and to do things together. Besides, my girl friends just do not go out much without their husbands.

What do you suggest?

2. Our wedding is only one week away, so please reply promptly. We finally got around to talking about children seriously the other night, and Jim said straight out that he does not want children for at least three or four years. He maintains we deserve this kind of freedom "before we are tied down with kids."

I frankly don't see children as a burden. These days, with a little planning, you can fit them right into your social life, travel, and almost anything. Money is no problem, and I am afraid of the attitude that says you have to have everything nailed down and secure before you have a baby. We've both been around a good deal, and I for one am more than ready to start a family. What do you think?

3. About the only thing that bugs me about my fiancé is that he makes no plans.

When he calls, the second sentence out of his mouth is always, "What do you want to do?" Then I say, "I don't know," and we waste time floundering around and end up irritated and doing nothing. It just seems stupid!

I think it's the man's reponsibility to think up things and make definite suggestions and plans. He says there just are not that many things he likes to do, and that I like to move around too much.

I'm afraid his attitude could make for a lot of boredom in marriage. What should I do?

4. My wife is Mrs. Clean. She's forever dusting, mopping, and straightening . . . Any spill, rip, tear, or wrinkle is a crisis.

Now, I've always thought of myself as a neat person. But, if I skip a shoeshine or a shave on a weekend, wear the same shorts or socks two days running, leave a match on the floor, miss using enough deodorant, or drop a jacket on a chair instead of hanging it up—it's war! I'm all for comfort. There are a lot more things in life than cleanliness. Whoever said, "Cleanliness is next to Godliness," was a heretic! How can I straighten her out?

5. If my mother-in-law makes one more comment on my cooking or housekeeping, I think I will scream. She has nothing to do at all so she drops in two or three times a week and tells me what's wrong with my recipes, why I should change furniture polish, how the plant won't grow in that corner, and why I shouldn't spend money on having laundry done. There is never a word that comes out of her mouth that isn't some direct or implied criticism.

I keep telling John to shape her up on this matter. He says he knows his mother can sometimes be a pain but that I am too sensitive too. Besides, he adds, I'm a big girl and can fight my own battles. What do you suggest?

God's Word: Wait Until Marriage[16]

A. Both adultery (sexual intercourse between a married man and a woman not his wife, or between a married woman and a man not her husband) and fornication (sexual intercourse between any two people not married to each other) are condemned in Scripture.

1. Adultery is prohibited expressly in the Ten Commandments (Exod. 20:14) and is condemned in many other passages in the Old Testament. (See Gen. 20:3; Prov. 6:32-33; Jer. 5:7-8.)
2. Jesus repeated the commandment prohibiting adultery

(Mark 10:19) and even added that looking upon a woman to lust after her amounts to the commission of adultery with her in one's heart (Matt. 5:27-28). He condemned both adultery and fornication in Mark 7:20-23. (See also Mark 10:11-12).

3. One of the few "essentials" that the apostles felt necessary to touch upon in their letter to the Antioch Christians was that they abstain from fornication (Acts 15:28-29).

4. Paul speaks out strongly against sex outside of marriage in many of his letters. For example:

   a. 1 Corinthians 6:9-20. Paul warns us that those who continue to practice fornication or adultery "shall not inherit the kingdom of God" (vv. 9-10). He adds that "our bodies are not for sexual immorality, but for the Lord" (v. 13). Indeed, our bodies are "members of Christ" (v. 15) and "temples of the Holy Spirit" who is in us (v. 19). Accordingly, we are to glorify God in our bodies (v. 20) by fleeing sexual immorality (v. 18).

   b. Galatians 5:19-21. Sexual immorality, impurity, sensuality, and carousings are all included in Paul's list of the "deeds of the flesh," the doers of which "shall not inherit the kingdom of God." We are to display the fruit of the Holy Spirit, which includes love, patience, faithfulness, and self-control (vv. 22-23).

   c. Ephesians 5:3-12. Paul urges the Ephesian Christians not to let sexual immorality or impurity "even be named" among them (v. 3). Moreover, they are not to participate in the "unfruitful deeds of darkness," and they are to expose and reprove them (v. 11).

   d. See also Romans 13:9, 1 Corinthians 5:9-11; 10:8; 2 Corinthians 12:21, Colossians 3:5-7; 1 Thessalonians 4:1-8; 2 Timothy 2:22.

5. Other New Testament authors were equally emphatic in their condemnation of sex outside of marriage. Hebrews 13:4; James 2:11; 2 Peter 2:9-16; Jude 7; Revelation 2:20-22; 9:21.

B. A biblical figure who "fled" from sexual immorality is Joseph (see Gen. 39:7-12). His master's wife asked him repeatedly, day after day, to lie with her, but Joseph refused each time: "How then could I do this great evil, and sin against God?" (v. 9). One day when he was doing his work around the house, she caught him by his garment and asked him again. Understanding the seriousness of this temptation, Joseph "left his garment in her hand and fled, and went outside" (v. 12).

BENEFITS OF WAITING UNTIL MARRIAGE

A. No guilt. God tells us to wait until marriage. Not waiting will create guilt that will hamper your relationships with Him, with your sexual partner, and with everyone else. By waiting you can know, because God says so, that Jesus Christ smiles on your marriage bed.

B. No fear. Waiting insures that you will never have to be afraid, not even to the extent of one fleeting thought, of having to build a marriage on an unexpected pregnancy.

C. No comparison. Waiting insures that you will never fall into the devastating trap of comparing your spouse's sexual performance with that of a previous sexual partner.

D. Spiritual growth. On the positive side, waiting will help you subject your physical drives to the lordship of Christ, and thereby develop your self-control, an important aspect of the fruit of the Holy Spirit. Also, if you get married and are later separated temporarily (e.g., for a business trip), then this discipline early in your relationship will give both of you confidence and trust in each other during that time of separation.

E. Greater joy. Waiting insures that there will be something saved for your marriage relationship, for that first night and for the many nights thereafter. The anticipation of the fulfillment of your relationship in sexual union is exciting. Don't spoil it by jumping the gun.

HOW FAR SHALL WE GO BEFORE MARRIAGE?

Given our conviction to refrain from sexual intercourse until marriage, the question remains: How far shall we go, short of sexual intercourse, before marriage?

A. The answer to this question depends upon how far along you are in your relationship together (first date or engaged) and upon your abilities to withstand the very strong temptation to have sexual intercourse.

B. However, a general principle which we feel applies to

everyone is the following: That which has its natural end in sexual intercourse should be held to your wedding night.

1. This means, at the very least, that heavy petting, direct stimulation of each other's sexual organs, and mutual masturbation should be out. Don't build up your sexual drives and desires to the point of no return, lest your physical relationship become a source of frustration rather than of joy for you.

2. This also means that you should not engage in any physical activity which will build up the other person's sexual drives to the point of no return. In the context of a different problem, that of eating certain types of food, Paul puts forth the general exhortation that we not do anything which causes our brother (or sister) to stumble (see Rom. 12:13,21). Thus, both persons must be sensitive to each other and must place the other's spiritual health ahead of their own desire for physical fulfillment now. When in doubt, don't! For "whatever is not from faith is sin" (Rom. 14:23). Pray, alone and together, about your physical relationship. If you can't visualize Jesus Christ smiling at the two of you, the Holy Spirit may be urging you to pull back the reins a little, for the sake of your love for the Lord and for each other.

C. This does not mean that the two of you are not going to relate physically before marriage, nor does it mean that your sexual drives will not increase as you do relate physically. And it certainly does not mean that you will not want to go to bed with each other. But it does mean that the two of you will make Jesus Christ the Lord of your sexual life and that you are going to wait for the green light from Him.

YOUR FIRST YEAR BUDGET[17]

(Try to figure out your expenses for the first twelve months of marriage.)

Flexible Expenses
Clothing	$ _____
Furniture and Equipment, including repairs	_____
Medical and Dental Care	_____
Contributions to Charity	_____
Gifts, Entertainment, Recreation, Hobbies	_____

Day-to-Day Living Costs   _____
  Food and Household Supplies   _____
  Laundry and Cleaning   _____
  Books, Papers, Magazines   _____
  Drug Store Sundries   _____
  Car Upkeep   _____
  Personal Allowances   _____
    Total Flexible Expenses $_____
    Add all flexible expenses and divide by 12.
    This is the amount you need set aside each
    month to take care of flexible expenses.

Fixed Expenses
  Paycheck deductions for Taxes $_____
                 Social Security   _____
                 Other   _____
  Housing—Rent   _____
         Mortgage Payments   _____
         Taxes, Special Assessments   _____
  Utilities—Gas   _____
         Electric   _____
         Phone   _____
         Water   _____
  Church Support—Sunday Collections   _____
               Special Collections   _____
  Union or Professional Association Dues _____
  Membership Fees in Organizations   _____
  Insurance Premiums   _____
  Vehicle Licenses   _____
  Regular Payments—Loans   _____
                Installments   _____
                Christmas Savings Club _____
                Other   _____
  Regular Savings   _____
  Add *Total Fixed Expenses* $_____
  Then divide by 12—this is the amount you will need to
  set aside each month to take care of fixed expenses.
(1) Figure out your total income for your first year of
     marriage.
     (Total Annual Income) $_____
(2) Add your yearly flexible expenses and fixed
     expenses.
     (Total Annual Expenses) $_____

Deduct (2) from (1) to find out if you are in the black or red.

_____

WHAT IS YOUR OPINION?[18]

Agree   Disagree

_____   _____   1. It is all right to modify the truth to avoid unpleasantness in the home.

_____   _____   2. An argument is a destructive force in married life.

_____   _____   3. Quarreling is always wrong for a Christian couple even though insights are gained thereby.

_____   _____   4. Every couple should have friends with whom they can talk over their marital problems and adjustments.

_____   _____   5. The wisest course to take when an argument seems to be developing is to remain silent or leave the room.

_____   _____   6. When a Christian couple are at an impasse in their discussion or communication, the best solution is to pray together about their differences.

_____   _____   7. It is sometimes necessary to nag another person in order to get him to respond.

_____   _____   8. There are certain matters about marriage that are best not discussed by a couple.

_____   _____   9. The Bible teaches that we should avoid people who get angry much of the time.

_____   _____   10. Only positive feelings should be expressed in the marriage relationship.

_____   _____   11. If we are married and something our mate does bothers us, we should go ahead and tell him or her and try to change him or her.

_____ _____ 12. It is a sign of spiritual and emotional immaturity for a person to be angry at another
individual.

FINANCES QUESTIONNAIRE

Circle the answer describing how you feel about the following:

E—Extra
D—Desirable
U—Useful
N—Necessary

Life Insurance	E	D	U	N
A Color TV	E	D	U	N
New Furniture	E	D	U	N
A Stereo Set	E	D	U	N
A Wig	E	D	U	N
Having a Car	E	D	U	N
Having Two Cars	E	D	U	N
Owning a Boat	E	D	U	N
Planning a Family Budget	E	D	U	N
Owning Your Own Home within Five Years	E	D	U	N
Giving 10% to the Church	E	D	U	N
A Dishwasher	E	D	U	N
A Blender	E	D	U	N
Laundry Service	E	D	U	N
A Camper	E	D	U	N
Pets	E	D	U	N
A Complete Set of China	E	D	U	N
Donations to Charity	E	D	U	N
A Working Wife	E	D	U	N
Vacation Once a Year	E	D	U	N
Air Conditioner	E	D	U	N
Continued Formal Education After Marriage	E	D	U	N
Long Term Savings Plan	E	D	U	N
Medical Insurance	E	D	U	N
Credit Cards	E	D	U	N
Installment Buying	E	D	U	N
A Motorcycle	E	D	U	N
Beauty Shop Once a Week	E	D	U	N

DEALING WITH IN-LAWS[19]

The following suggestions by Landis and Landis could provide
guidelines for couples in relation to their in-laws:

1. Treat your in-laws with the same consideration and respect that you give to friends who are not in-laws.
2. When in-laws take an interest in your life and give advice, do just as you would if any friend gave advice: if it is good, follow it; if it is not good, accept it graciously and then ignore it.
3. Remember that many times when the in-laws appear to be too concerned with your affairs, they are not trying to interfere in your life but are sincerely interested in your welfare.
4. Look for the good points in your in-laws.
5. When you visit your in-laws, make the visits reasonably short.
6. When visiting in-laws, be as thoughtful, courteous, and helpful as you are when you are visiting other friends.
7. Accept your in-laws as they are; remember that they would probably like to make changes in you, too.
8. Mothers-in-law have been close to their children before marriage; give them time to find new interests in life.
9. Go into marriage with a positive attitude toward your in-laws— you believe it is a good family to marry into and you intend to enjoy your new family.
10. Give advice to your in-laws only if they ask for it; even then, use self-restraint.
11. Discuss the faults of your spouse only with him, not with your family.
12. Do not quote your family or hold them up as models to your spouse.
13. Remember that it takes at least two people to create an in-law problem. No one person is ever entirely to blame.

For a married couple to handle relationships with parents and in-laws on a positive basis, they need to:[20]

1. Be mindful of the fact that family ties are normal, necessary, and important and that a brusque rejection of them can only bring unhappiness to all;
2. Make the process of separating themselves gradual rather than abrupt;
3. Accept the spouse's concern for his parental family;
4. Accept the fact that parents cannot automatically stop being interested in, and concerned about, their children just because the latter get married, and that parental help can sometimes be a wonderful thing to have;
5. Present a united front to any attempt by parents or in-laws to interfere; firmness is more effective than hostility.

THOUGHTS AND PRINCIPLES ABOUT IN-LAWS[21]

The main facts about in-law tensions are as follows:

1. The person who causes most of these conflicts is unfortunately the mother-in-law. One study found that she initiated as much trouble as all the other in-laws put together.
2. Victims of in-law interference are nearly always the daughters-in-law. Often the mother-in-law is jealous of her daughter-in-law for dividing the affection of her son and tries to win back the central position in his life by alienating him from his wife.
3. Competition and conflict between these two women reaches its most violent form when they have to live together in the same house.
4. Rearing of the children is frequently another area in which the mother-in-law interferes.
5. A mother-in-law who acts in these ways can be very troublesome. But she deserves your pity more than your hostility. What this person really needs is the love of those around her, but since she seems unable to get it she tries instead to gain her ends by manipulation and intrigue. Unfortunately she usually does not realize that she is completely defeating her own purpose.

Principles to follow with in-laws:

1. No in-law interference can damage a sound marriage. In-laws cannot drive a wedge between husband and wife who stand firm together.
2. The policy to adopt is to make it clear that you want to be friendly and you want to work for harmony between the generations, but you will not tolerate unwarranted interference in your marriage. This must be made clear with no compromise.
3. A confrontation or discussion should be followed up by sincere and genuine attempts to be friendly and conciliatory. You can behave lovingly towards them even if you don't feel loving, and the action tends to promote the feeling. It will help and encourage your spouse if you make a real effort in this direction. Experience shows that this policy can, in time, achieve a surprising degree of success.
4. If you and your in-laws really have very little in common, short visits from time to time are best.
5. Remember family ties cannot be broken, and they last throughout a lifetime. Even if your relationships with your in-laws are not as they should be right now, a time may come when you may need their help or they may need yours.

SAMPLE WEDDING VOWS[22]

I, Ronald, take you, Carolyn, to be my lawfully wedded wife. I promise to love and honor you, using as my example the love which Christ has for the Church in that He loved her and gave Himself for her. I promise to take you into my home and to provide for your material needs; to bring you affection and cheer, understanding and companionship; to be to you a source of strength; and to render to you all that is rightfully due a wife from her husband. I promise to do these things with all my energies, whether for better or worse, in sickness or in health, in riches or in poverty, according to God's holy ordinance, and forsaking all others, to give myself only and always to you, until death itself parts us.

I, Carolyn, take you, Ronald, to be my lawfully wedded husband. I promise to love and honor you and be subject to you as unto the Lord, to be a help meet to you, to provide those things in our home which are necessary for your happiness and comfort; to bring you affection and encouragement, understanding and companionship, and to render to you all that is rightfully due a husband from his wife. I promise to do these things with all my energies whether for better or for worse, in sickness or in health, in riches or in poverty, according to God's holy ordinance, and forsaking all others, to give myself only and always to you until death itself parts us. "Entreat me not to leave you, nor to return from following you. For where you go, I will go, and where you lodge I will lodge. Your people shall be my people, and your God, my God."

The exchange of rings:

With this ring, I take you to be my wife and endow you with all my earthly goods. I give it as a token of our mutual vows and of my love for you. The ring is circular, having neither beginning nor end. My love for you did have a beginning, but by God's grace, it will never have an end. In the name of the Father, and of the Son, and of the Holy Spirit, Amen.

With this ring, I take you to be my husband. I give it as a token of our mutual vows and of my love for you. The ring is gold, long the most precious of metals, and I give it as a symbol of the pricelessness in God's sight of the oneness He has created between us. In the name of the Father, and of the Son, and of the Holy Spirit, Amen.

YOU PAID HOW MUCH FOR THAT?[23]

Secret thoughts of a husband: "I just can't understand why my wife is always short of money. Now if I took over, things would be more efficient and there would be money to spare."

A wife broods: "I don't know why my husband says he can't take me out more often. His expenses aren't that high."

Do you confess to thinking like that occasionally? Here is your chance to show how much you know about the day-to-day money problems your spouse faces. This quiz for married couples is divided into two sections, one for each partner. Each of you is asked the approximate cost of twenty-five items or services that the other usually pays for. Here are the rules:

Wives ask their husbands the questions headed "For Men." Husbands ask their wives the questions headed "For Women." In some cases a price range rather than the approximate cost may be allowed.

Score four points for each correct answer. Don't be too strict. Give your spouse credit for a correct answer if he or she comes within, say, 10 percent of the right amount.

If you want to compare scores, go ahead. But that's not the point of the quiz. The idea is simply to show you how well you understand your mate's side of the spending. And maybe the quiz will teach you a lesson: Don't beef about somebody's spending habits until you know what you are talking about.

For Men

How much would you have to pay for these?

1. A ten-pound turkey _____
2. A five-pound bag of potatoes _____
3. A chocolate cake mix _____
4. A chuck roast for six _____
5. A week's supply of milk _____
6. A broom _____
7. A large box of detergent _____
8. A two-quart ceramic casserole with lid _____
9. A set of eight water glasses _____
10. A set of six steak knives _____
11. A fake fur coat _____
12. A pair of pantyhose _____
13. A three-piece polyester pants suit _____
14. A woman's swimsuit _____
15. A girl's blouse _____
16. A pair of kid's jeans _____
17. A pair of children's shoes _____
18. A nylon lace half slip _____
19. A king-size no-iron sheet _____
20. A machine-washable, drip-dry tablecloth _____
21. 3½ yards of double-knit fabric _____
22. A pair of steel sewing shears _____
23. A pair of sheer Dacron window curtains _____
24. A permanent wave _____
25. A tube of lipstick _____

For Women

How much would you pay for these?

1. A quart of motor oil _____
2. A chassis lubrication _____
3. A set of shock absorbers _____

4. A pair of first-line tires
5. A 20-inch power mower   ———
6. Fertilizer to cover the lawn   ———
7. A 6-foot aluminum stepladder   ———
8. A set of four screwdrivers   ———
9. An adjustable wrench   ———
10. A gallon of latex paint   ———
11. A fiber glass fishing rod   ———
12. A boy's baseball mitt   ———
13. A haircut, including tip   ———
14. The home heating bill for a year   ———
15. The yearly federal income tax   ———
16. Your husband's annual life insurance premiums   ———
17. An 'off-the-rack' worsted suit   ———
18. A man's raincoat   ———
19. A medium-priced pair of shoes   ———
20. A pair of knit slacks   ———
21. A wash-and-wear shirt   ———
22. Ten shares of American Tel & Tel   ———
23. Dinner for four at a good restaurant, including tip   ———
24. A businessman's lunch for two   ———
25. Two tickets to a football or baseball game   ———

Family Communication Guidelines

Job 19:2; Proverbs 18:21; 25:11; James 3:8-10; 1 Peter 3:10

1. Be a ready listener and do not answer until the other person has finished talking (Proverbs 18:13; James 1:19).

2. Be slow to speak. Think first. Don't be hasty in your words. Speak in such a way that the other person can understand and accept what you say (Proverbs 15:23, 28; 21:23; 29:20; James 1:19).

3. Speak the truth always, but do it in love. Do not exaggerate (Ephesians 4:15, 25; Colossians 3:9).

4. Do not use silence to frustrate the other person. Explain why you are hesitant to talk at this time.

5. Do not become involved in quarrels. It is possible to disagree without quarreling (Proverbs 17:14; 20:3; Romans 13:13; Ephesians 4:31).

6. Do not respond in anger. Use a soft and kind response (Proverbs 14:29, 15:1; 25:15; 29:11; Ephesians 4:26, 31).

7. When you are in the wrong, admit it and ask for forgiveness (James 5:16). When someone confesses to you, tell him you forgive him. Be sure it is *forgotten* and not brought up to the person (Proverbs 17:9; Ephesians 4:32; Colossians 3:13; 1 Peter 4:8).

8. Avoid nagging (Proverbs 10:19; 17:9).

9. Do not blame or criticize the other but restore him, encourage him, and edify him (Romans 14:13; Galatians 6:1; 1 Thessalonians 5:11). If someone verbally attacks, criticizes, or blames you, do not respond in the same manner (Romans 12:17, 21; 1 Peter 2:23; 3:9).

10. Try to understand the other person's opinion. Make allowances for differences. Be concerned about their interests (Philippians 2:1-4; Ephesians 4:2).

NOTES

1. Robert K. Kelley, *Courtship, Marriage and the Family* (New York: Harcourt, Brace & World, 1969), pp. 212-13. Used by permission.
2. Lyle B. Gangsei, *Manual for Group Pre-Marital Counseling* (New York: Association Press, 1971), pp. 56-57. Used by permission.
3. David Knox, *Marriage—Who? When? Why?* (Englewood Cliffs, N.J.: Prentice-Hall, 1975), pp. 101-2. Used by permission.
4. James R. Hine, *Your Marriage Analysis and Renewal* (Danville, Ill.: Interstate Publishers and Printers, 1966), pp. 19-20, adapted.
5. Richard Udry, *The Social Context of Marriage*, 3d ed. (New York: Lippincott, 1974), p. 265.
6. Data Track Research Services Institute of Life Insurance, New York. No. 1 Women, Summer 1974, p. 3.
7. Letha Scanzoni and Nancy Hardesty, *All We're Meant to Be* (Waco, Tex.: Word, 1974), p. 197. Adapted.
8. Ibid., p. 198. Adapted.
9. Udry, p. 305. Adapted.
10. Ibid., p. 304. Adapted.
11. Ibid., pp. 305-7. Adapted.
12. Robert Kelley, *Courtship, Marriage and the Family*, 2d ed. (New York: Harcourt, Brace, Jovanovich, 1974), pp. 367-68. Adapted.
13. Udry, pp. 307-8. Adapted.
14. Ibid.
15. Adapted from *Marriage: Discoveries and Encounters*, The Cana Conference of Chicago, pp. 11-12.
16. Adapted from *Lutheran Youth Alive Newsletter.*
17. H. Norman Wright, *The Christian Faces . . . Emotions, Marriage, and Family Relationships* (Denver, Colo.: Christian Marriage Enrichment, 1975), pp. 80-81.
18. H. Norman Wright, *Communication—Key to Your Marriage*, Leader's Manual (Glendale, Calif.: Gospel Light, 1974), p. 31.
19. Judson T. Landis and Mary G. Landis, *Personal Adjustment, Marriage and Family Living* (Englewood Cliffs, N.J.: Prentice-Hall, 1966), pp. 238-39.
20. Norman Lobsenz and Clark Blackburn, *How to Stay Married* (New York: Cowles, 1968), pp. 55-56.
21. Udry, 288-93. Adapted.
22. Written by Ron and Carolyn Klaus, now of Philadelphia, for their wedding in June 1968.
23. Reprinted by permission from *Changing Times*, The Kiplinger Magazine (June 1972). Copyright 1972 by The Kiplinger Washington Editors, Inc., 1729 H Street, N.W., Washington, D.C. 20006.

T-JTA Resources
and Scriptures

A. NERVOUS

1. Gockel, Herman. *Answer to Anxiety.* St. Louis: Concordia, 1965.
2. Hauck, Paul H. *Overcoming Worry and Fear.* Philadelphia: Westminster, 1975.
3. Lee, Earl G. *Recycled for Living.* Glendale, Calif.: Gospel Light, Regal, 1973.
4. Lloyd-Jones, D. Martyn. *Spiritual Depression: Its Causes and Cures.* (Chapters 8, 10, 11.) Grand Rapids: Eerdmans, 1965.
5. Seamands, David. "How Jesus Handled His Emotions."*
6. _____. "God's Prescription for Life's Greatest Fears."*
7. _____. "Damaged Emotions."*
8. Wright, H. Norman. *An Answer to Worry and Anxiety.* Irvine, Calif.: Harvest, 1976.
9. _____. "Handling Worry and Anxiety."†
10. Psalm 131:2   John 16:33   Hebrews 13:6
    Isaiah 26:3   Romans 5:1; 15:13   1 Peter 5:7
    Matthew 6:34; 11:28   Philippians 4:6-7   1 John 4:18

B. DEPRESSIVE

1. Cammer, Leonard. *Up from Depression.* New York: Pocket Books, 1971.
2. Flach, Frederic. *The Secret Strength of Depression.* New York: Lippincott, 1971.
3. Hauck, Paul H. *Overcoming Depression.* Philadelphia: Westminster, 1973.
4. Lloyd-Jones, D. Martyn. *Spiritual Depression: Its Causes and Cures.* New York: Pocket Books, 1965.
5. Kraines, Samuel, and Thetford, Eloise. *Help for the Depressed.* Springfield, Ill.: C. C. Thomas, 1972.
6. Seamands, David. "How Jesus Handled His Emotions."*
7. _____. "God's Prescription for Life's Greatest Fears."*

8. ————. "Damaged Emotions."*
9. ————. "The Spirit of a Person."*
10. ————. "The Hidden Tormentors."*
11. Wright, H. Norman. *An Answer to Depression.* Irvine, Calif.: Harvest, 1976.
12. ————. "Can Anything Good Come Out of Anger or Depression?"⁺
13. ————. *The Christian Use of Emotional Power.* Old Tappan, N.J.: Revell, 1974.
14. Job 4:6
    Psalm 3:5-6; 40:1-2; 42:5, 11; 43:5; 147:3
    Proverbs 14:30
    Matthew 12:20
    Luke 4:18

C. ACTIVE SOCIAL AND

D. EXPRESSIVE RESPONSIVE

1. Augsburger, David. *Caring Enough to Confront.* Glendale, Calif.: Gospel Light, Regal, 1975.
2. Nirenberg, Jesse S. *Getting Through to People.* Englewood Cliffs, N.J.: Prentice-Hall, 1968.
3. Powell, John. *Why Am I Afraid to Love?* Niles, Ill.: Argus, 1967.
4. ————. *"Why Am I Afraid to Tell You Who I Am?* Niles, Ill.: Argus, 1969.
5. Seamands, David. "Wishing, Wanting and Willing."*
6. ————. "Is Everyday Halloween for You?"*
7. Wright, H. Norman. *Communication—Key to Your Marriage.* Glendale, Calif.: Gospel Light, Regal, 1974.
8. ————. "Communication—Key to Your Marriage."⁺ (Tape series)
9. Zunin, Leonard. *Contact—The First Four Minutes.* New York: Ballantine, 1974.
10. 2 Timothy 1:7   James 5:16

E. SYMPATHETIC

1. Becker, Wilhard. *Love in Action.* Grand Rapids: Zondervan, 1969.
2. Bisagno, John. *Love Is Something You Do.* New York: Harper & Row, 1975.
3. Buscaglia, Leo. *Love.* Thorofare, N.J.: Slack, 1973.
4. Powell, John. *The Secret of Staying in Love.* Niles, Ill.: Argus, 1974.
5. ————. *Why Am I Afraid to Love?* Niles, Ill.: Argus, 1967.
6. 1 Samuel 12:23; 23:21   Ephesians 4:31-32
   Romans 12:10, 15; 14:19; 15:1   Hebrews 2:18; 4:15-16
   1 Corinthians 13   1 John 4:7
   Galatians 6:2

F. SUBJECTIVE

1. Keyes, Kenneth S. *Taming Your Mind.* (Orig. title, *How to Develop Your Thinking Ability.*) Berkeley: Living Love, 1975.
2. Lembo, John. *Help Yourself.* Niles, Ill.: Argus, 1974.
3. Missildine, W. Hugh. *Your Inner Child of the Past.* New York: Simon & Schuster, 1963.
4. Schmidt, Jerry, *You Can Help Yourself,* Irvine, Calif.: Harvest, 1978.
5. Seamands, David. "Is Your God Fit to Love?"*
6. _____. "The Hidden Child in Us All."*
7. _____. "The Healing of Memories."*
8. _____. "My Grace Is Sufficient for You."*
9. Wright, H. Norman. *The Christian Use of Emotional Power.* Old Tappan, N.J.: Revell, 1974.
10. Psalm 119:66   Philippians 1:27; 2:5; 4:8-9
    1 Corinthians 9:27   Colossians 1:10
    2 Corinthians 13:5   1 Peter 1:14

G. DOMINANT OR SUBMISSIVE

1. Ahlem, Lloyd H. *Do I Have to Be Me?* Glendale, Calif.: Gospel Light, Regal, 1973.
2. Augsburger, David. *Caring Enough to Confront.* Glendale, Calif.: Gospel Light, Regal, 1973.
3. Hoekema, Anthony A. *The Christian Looks at Himself.* Grand Rapids: Eerdmans, 1975.
4. Jabay, Earl. *The God Players.* Grand Rapids: Zondervan, 1970.
5. Lembo, John. *Help Yourself.* Niles, Ill.: Argus, 1974.
6. Maltz, Maxwell. *Magic Power of Self-Image Psychology: The New Way to a Bright Full Life.* Englewood Cliffs, N.J.: Prentice-Hall, 1964.
7. Narramore, Bruce, and Counts, Bill. *Guilt and Freedom.* Irvine, Calif.: Harvest House, 1974.
8. Narramore, Bruce. "Guilt and Self-Image." Forest Falls, Calif.: First Evangelical Free Church, 1975.
9. Smith, Manuel. *When I Say No, I Feel Guilty.* New York: Bantam, 1975.
10. Swindoll, Charles. "Lessons Learned from Failure."*
11. Wright, H. Norman. "The Christian Faces Emotions, Marriage, and Family Relationships."*

H. HOSTILE

1. Hauck, Paul H. *Overcoming Frustration and Anger.* Philadelphia: Westminster, 1973.
2. Carlson, Dwight, *Overcoming Hurts and Anger.* Eugene, Ore.: Harvest House, 1981.

3. Wright, H. Norman. *An Answer to Frustration and Anger.* Irvine, Calif.: Harvest House, 1977.
4. ————. "Can Anything Good Come Out of Anger or Depression?"†
5. ————. *The Christian Use of Emotional Power.* Old Tappan, N.J.: Revell, 1974.
6. Psalm 4:4
   Proverbs 14:29; 15:1, 18; 16:32; 29:11
   Ecclesiastes 7:7-9
   Matthew 5:22
   Romans 12:19; 14:13
   Ephesians 4:26, 31-32
   Colossians 3:8, 10
   James 1:19

I. SELF-DISCIPLINED

1. Carlson, Dwight. *Run and Not Be Weary.* Old Tappan, N.J.: Revell, 1974.
2. Lembo, John. *Help Yourself.* Niles, Ill.: Argus, 1974.
3. Missildine, W. Hugh. *Your Inner Child of the Past.* Chapters 13 and 14. New York: Simon & Schuster, 1963.
4. Oates, Wayne. *Confessions of a Workaholic.* Nashville: Abingdon, 1972.
5. Swindoll, Charles. "Lessons Learned from Failure."‡
6. Proverbs 14:17   Titus 2:2
   Romans 11:12   Hebrews 10:36
   1 Corinthians 9:27; 14:40; 15:58   James 1:4; 5:7
   Galatians 5:22-24   1 Peter 1:13-15
   Philippians 3:14; 4:13

J. GUILT

1. Jabay, Earl. *The God Players,* Grand Rapids: Zondervan, 1970.
2. Narramore, Bruce, and Counts, Bill. *Guilt and Freedom.* Irvine, Calif.: Harvest House, 1962.
3. Seamands, David. "Damaged Emotions."*
4. ————. "The Spirit of a Person."*
5. ————. "The Hidden Tormentors."*
6. ————. "Is Your God Fit to Love?"*
7. ————. "The Hidden Child in Us All."*
8. ————. "The Healing of Memories."*
9. ————. "My Grace Is Sufficient for You."*
10. ————. "Wishing, Wanting and Willing."*
11. ————. "Is Everyday Halloween for You?"*
12. Tournier, Paul. *Guilt and Grace.* New York: Harper & Row, 1962.

K. FORGIVENESS

1. Augsburger, David. *The Freedom of Forgiveness.* Chicago: Moody, 1973.
2. Linn, M. L., and Linn, D. *Healing of Memories.* Paramus, N.J.: Paulist, 1975.
3. Seamands, David. "Love, Honor and Forgiveness."*

*Order tapes by David Seamands from Tape Ministries, P.O. Box 3389, Pasadena, CA 91103.
†Order tapes by H. Norman Wright from Christian Marriage Enrichment, 8000 E. Girard, Suite 206, Denver, CO 80231.
‡Order tapes by Charles Swindoll from the First Evangelical Free Church, 643 Malvern, Fullerton, CA 92732.

Moody Press, a ministry of the Moody Bible Institute, is designed for education, evangelization, and edification. If we may assist you in knowing more about Christ and the Christian life, please write us without obligation: Moody Press, c/o MLM, Chicago, Illinois 60610.

97021

Overton Memorial Library
Premarital counseling /
362.8286 W949p 1981

97021